TOMORROW'S LANGUAGE

ALSO BY HELEN MARSHALL

Hair Side, Flesh Side
Gifts for the One Who Comes After
The Migration
The Gold Leaf Executions

TOMORROW'S LANGUAGE

DR. HELEN MARSHALL

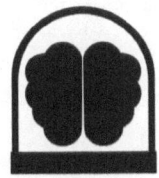

Brain Jar Press
PO Box 6687
Upper Mt Gravatt, QLD, 4122
Australia
www.BrainJarPress.com

Copyright © 2023 by Helen Marshall.

The moral right of Helen Marshall to be identified as the author of this work has been asserted.

All rights reserved. No part of this book may be reproduced in any form or by any electronic or mechanical means, including information storage and retrieval systems, without written permission from the author, except for the use of brief quotations in a book review.

Cover design by Vince Haig

ISBN: 978-1-922479-63-1 (Ebook) | 978-1-922479-62-4 (Paperback)

For Nina Allan

CONTENTS

The Only Lights are Headlights	1
Sex, Death and the Man-Omelet in 'The Specialist's Hat'	10
Survival Strategies	20
Survival Strategies for Weird Times	42
'A Flare of Light or The Great Clomping Foot of Nerdism?'	54
On Last Year's Language	80
Bibliography	91
About the Author	97

THE ONLY LIGHTS ARE HEADLIGHTS

First published in *Weird Fiction Review*. August 10, 2016.

When I was twelve years old, I was afraid — desperately, morbidly afraid — of horror flicks. My best friend in grade seven was a girl named Steph Melnychuk. We played softball together back in Sarnia — a small town in Ontario maybe double the size of Bangor where Stephen King grew up — and her throw was something to be reckoned with. I was the only one willing to catch for her (badly at that) and I still remember the hot sting when the ball went blazing into my clumsy glove. She was taller than me by about five inches, smart, effortlessly cool. She liked to throw slumber parties at which we'd dance to Michael Jackson's 'Thriller,' and one night on a dare we locked ourselves in the basement bathroom to paint our faces with glow-in-the-dark nail polish. But it was her idea, her deep-seated love of the macabre.

She was the horror fan, not me.

In the early 1990s, Steph invited me over to watch a made-for-TV flick called *Sometimes They Come Back* in which a reluctant high school teacher returns to his hometown only to be harassed by the ghosts of the school kids that killed his brother. I was nervous from the get-go, and true to form the thing — schlocky as it was — stayed with me. In a recent conversation, the writer Sam J. Miller suggested that every horror writer has a personal monster, something that scares the bejesus out of them. For me, that monster is — and always has been — the ghost. Ghosts are like a warning about mortality, and at twelve years old I was only just beginning to grapple with those fears. No one in my family had died. I had never been to a funeral. The idea of dying fascinated me: it was repellent, awful, but it wasn't *unnatural*. Precisely the opposite.

That was my first experience with Stephen King.

In *Danse Macabre*, King lays out his theories surrounding the purposes and practices of writing horror:

> Terror — what Hunter Thompson calls 'fear and loathing' — often arises from a pervasive sense of disestablishment; that things are in the unmaking. If that sense of unmaking is sudden and seems personal — if it hits you around the heart — then it lodges in the memory as a complete set.

What I experienced as a twelve-year old was a profound sense of the possibility of unmaking, the possibility that a bunch of kids a little bit older than me could do hideous things — that kids my age were vulnerable; they could be murdered, they could drown, they could be struck by trains that seemed to come out of nowhere.

When I was in my final year of high school, a tanker truck smashed into the side of my dad's car on an icy stretch of road within sight of the chemical plant where he worked. My mom was in South Africa at the time, clearing up the effects of my grandmother who had recently passed on, and my older brother Justin was living just outside of Toronto, a good three hours' drive away. So it was my younger sister and I who were driven to the hospital — I don't remember by whom — while my dad was in critical care. My dad had always had a definite vitality about him. He used to regale us with stories of his childhood growing up in Rhodesia where he set scorpions and matabele ants to fight; later, he barely missed an opportunity to be on the South African fencing team. He had, he told us, a pet chimpanzee. But when we saw him it was like meeting a stranger. He was badly bruised, black wires everywhere, and I couldn't make out much of what he was saying, only enough to know he didn't recognise me, not in that moment.

That moment brought about a sudden understanding that someone I loved could come undone. Could be *unmade*.

The power of ghosts is the power of memory, or at least that's what I've always thought. Memory is what gives us a sense of continuity, a sense of self. And ghosts are the most vital form of memory, just as haunting is really just a different kind of remembering.

My dad survived. The bruises healed. And although he was always frailer after that, prone to losing both his balance and his mental equilibrium as many who suffer traumatic head injuries were, I didn't lose him. But his memory suffered. Some part of that continuity — who he had been, who he was after — had shifted.

My second moment of unmaking occurred more recently. Six months ago I took up a permanent position at Anglia Ruskin University in Cambridge as Lecturer of Creative Writing and Publishing. It meant leaving Canada for good. But I had felt it was worth it. The job was a good one, a dream job in fact, and there were people I loved whom I didn't want to leave. I was prepared to make England my home.

But after my first semester had passed, a semester which had mostly masked for me the bitter campaign of misinformation and demagoguery that was raging in the background, the United Kingdom voted by a narrow margin to break away from the European Union. For those of my generation it had seemed an unthinkable outcome. Like so many others, I had gone to bed early that night, unwilling to watch another hour of political mayhem, feeling relatively secure that reason would prevail ... and the pre-voting polls had backed me up.

In *H is for Hawk*, the nature writer Helen MacDonald speaks about the origins of the word *bereavement* in the Old English *bereafian*, which means 'to deprive of, take away, seize, rob.' She writes that the death of her father felt like that:

Imagine your whole family is in a room. Yes, all of them. All the people you love. So then what happens is someone comes into the room and punches you all in the stomach. Each one of you. Really hard. So you're all on the floor. Right? So the thing is, you all share the same kind of pain, exactly the same, but you're too busy experiencing total agony to feel anything other than completely alone.

This image stuck with me on the day that Brexit was announced. It felt as if everyone I knew and loved had been damaged by what had happened — had been punched in the stomach — and yet I felt totally alone. I remember my partner telling me to come out for drinks in the city — to commiserate in company — but I didn't want to because I was crying and I wasn't sure if I could pull myself together enough to be presentable. And when I walked outside a week of grey skies and rain had perversely cleared to sunshine, so there were tourists walking along the canal; everything seemed strangely normal, and yet I couldn't shake the feeling that the world had changed irrevocably overnight. I felt untethered, unprepared for what was to come next.

The world has become a scary place. On July 14, less than two weeks before I wrote this, a 19-tonne cargo truck was driven into the crowds celebrating Bastille Day in Nice, France. Eighty-four people were killed. I don't like reading the news much right now.

King writes about a similar feeling after JFK's assassination, how those three days of grief which followed 'is perhaps the closest any people in history has ever come to a total period of mass consciousness and mass empathy and — in retrospect — mass memory.... Love cannot achieve that sort of across-the-board hammerstrike of emotion, apparently.'

But horror can. And that's the point, really.

As I write this, I'm sitting on a bus headed from Portland to Bangor for a research project about the publication of *Carrie* (1974), Stephen King's first novel. My own first novel was sold to Random House Canada this year, but that isn't what the project is about, only an excuse, really, to understand the origin of a writer whom I have come to respect and deeply admire.

The Hunt for Red October, streaked with static and all its buried Cold War anxieties, is playing on the overhead monitors, and outside everything is pure black. If the sun were shining, then perhaps I would recognise the landscape. Many do; there are fans who say that when they first enter Maine it has an instant recognisability, as if they're coming to a place they have always known. For me, it's a bit different. What hits me first are the smells, the thick scent of pine. My family used to vacation in nearby Kennebunk when I was a child.

They say that you're more likely to die in a car accident than in a terrorist attack.

I lied earlier, about my first encounter with Stephen King. Or rather, I misremembered.

I have a vague recollection: perched in the backseat of my parents' station wagon, someone was pointing into the distance, saying, 'That's where Stephen King lives.' My dad was driving. I felt completely safe. Untouchable. We had been fishing. I had got nothing but two-inch long feeders, but my brother kept telling me about how he had been going after a big one, a pike with crazy teeth set in a jagged old grin. I was seven or eight years old, I think. My brother was always telling me ghost stories, telling me whoppers. But I didn't believe them much. When you're that age it's still possible to feel completely safe.

Much of this is prelude, so forgive me. On to the matter at hand.

'The Man in the Black Suit' is typical in many respects of King's oeuvre. It's a good story, a solid story — so good, in fact, that it won the O. Henry prize in 1996. The narrative has a nostalgic quality to it; it is retrospective, a single memory that is offered up without explanation or even the hope of belief:

> I am now a very old man and this is something which happened to me when I was very young — only nine years old. It was 1914, the summer after my brother Dan died in the west field and three years before America got into World War I.... What I

might have done yesterday, who I might have seen here in my room at the nursing home, what I might have said to them or they to me ... those things are gone, but the face of the man in the black suit grows ever clearer, ever closer, and I remember every word he said.

It is a tale that is about transitions, about how life can slip away from you and how the grave is always waiting. King's writing has an undeniable charm to it. His stories drift along almost lazily, glinting with a touch of malice, maybe, but soothing too. His stories are like fish hooks, and once they catch you, struggle as you might, he'll reel you in all the same.

'Is horror art?' King asks in *Danse Macabre*. 'The work of horror can be nothing else; it achieves the level of art simply because it is looking for something beyond art, something that predates art.'

This particular story has always struck me as one of those which looks outward, beyond, *before*. As a narrative about an encounter with the Devil, it has a certain timeliness to it; yet King's Devil, despite his fancy suit, isn't urbane. He isn't a charmer. He's pure madness all the way through, and the tale he tells the narrator is perhaps one of the scariest of all: "Sad news, fisherboy,' he said. 'I've come with sad news.... Your mother is dead.'

What follows is a harrowing account in which the Devil taunts the narrator with a story about a fatal bee sting. The same allergy, the same weakness in the blood which had killed his brother Dan, was also shared by his mother, the Devil says, and that very day, only a few minutes ago, a bee flew through the window and caught her by surprise:

> 'You need to hear this, Gary; you need to hear this, my little fisherboy. It was your mother who passed that fatal weakness on to your brother Dan; you got some of it, but you also got a protection from your father that poor Dan somehow missed.... So, although I don't like to speak ill of the dead, it's almost a case of poetic justice, isn't it? After all, she killed your brother

Dan as surely as if she had put a gun to his head and pulled the trigger.'

The narrator resists, of course, but the tale is terrible precisely because it has the ring of truth. We've all inherited from our parents a terrible mortality. And at the same time the tale hooks deeply into the narrator's secret fear, the fear we all share about our loved ones: that while we were sleeping, while we weren't paying attention, something terrible might have happened....

In June, 1999, Stephen King was walking eight feet to the side of the road in North Lovell when a van hit and seriously injured him. He sustained an assortment of broken bones, a punctured lung, and a head injury. When I began reading *The Dead Zone* for the first time earlier this month, I was struck by the description of Johnny Smith in his coma. I had thought it was one of those filched autobiographical bits that often show up in King's work ('Write what you know', he says, and boy, does he!). But, of course, *The Dead Zone* was one of King's early novels, published in 1979, twenty years before the accident. And my point is not the supernatural but the *hyper*natural; after all, it's easy to imagine your own death when you're a horror writer. We do that kind of thing all the time.

The story is interesting in that it comes with very little moralizing. This is not a Devil eager to trick a man in order to steal his soul. The Devil here is malice, pure and simple; he is hunger; he is a grinning set of jaws that will devour you whole simply because you are there. It is old school religion, that, a religion of black and white in which the Devil comes, not because of a sin committed for which he might legitimately be feared, but simply because the Devil *is* and that is exactly what he does: he comes, and he comes, and he keeps on coming.

'The Man in the Black Suit' is a story about fishing; this is appropriate because fishing has such Biblical overtones, certainly, but also because it's a sport born half out of hunger and half out of playfulness. The narrator hooks himself a big one, a nineteen-inch brook trout. Quite the accomplishment for such a young boy. It is that fish alone that saves him, for it is enough to distract the Devil, who eats the thing whole with jaws that open up like a snake's.

In a recent interview following the publication of *Revival*, a Lovecraftian novel about a minister who loses his faith, King said he believed 'in evil', but he has for all his life 'gone back and forth about whether or not there's an outside evil, whether or not there's a force in the world that really wants to destroy us, from the inside out, individually and collectively.' The Devil of 'The Man in the Black Suit' is an outside force, but it isn't purely religious, to my mind, nor is he the accrual of bad forces, of crimes and transgressions, manifested in novels such as *Salem's Lot* (1975) or *It* (1986).

The Devil here is a kind of sudden badness that comes out of the blue.

Like a bee sting when you're allergic.

Like a truck coming out of nowhere in the darkness.

And there is a part of me that is thinking about this story as I sit on the bus, thinking about what it means to write about memory and to write about the fear of death. Outside, the world around me has fallen into darkness. I can't see my way clearly. Sometimes it seems as if the only lights are headlights.

Perhaps the end of the story isn't where we should be focusing. Because 'The Man in the Black Suit' ends as all horror stories end: with a tremor, with that sinking feeling of 'what comes next and do I really want to see?' But another way to look at the story is this: it's a fishing story, and all fishing stories are about lies, aren't they? Big whoppers. Tales that grow bigger in the telling.

And the Devil lied.

The narrator survived two World Wars, the atomic terror of the 60s, and God alone knows what personal tragedies that have come his way. He was born in 1905, and he has lived out his ninety years, suffering losses, yes, but living all the same. Maybe this fear has always been clawing at him, the image of that terrible grin like so many relentless headlights and the hungry words 'Biiig fiiish!' chasing all the truths of the moral world into ruin.

Except it is just a fear, a fear we all have.

Our man is still kicking, even after everything.

He may not be strong enough to run much more. He may not have fine large brook trout.

He may be old, and his creel may be empty.

But the Devil lies. And our man is still alive.

SEX, DEATH AND THE MAN-OMELET IN 'THE SPECIALIST'S HAT'

First published in *Weird Fiction Review*. September 9, 2015.

'The Specialist's Hat' has become a touchstone for a number of overlapping literary movements (magic realism, slipstream, interstitial, metafiction, fabulation, weird fiction), and there is good reason for this. It infuses tropes drawn from Gothic tales such as Horace Walpole's *Castle of Otranto* or ghost stories such as M. R. James's classic 'Oh, Whistle and I'll Come to You, My Lad' with a playfully postmodern sensibility. The story has a peculiar lightness to it, as it weaves together children's games, fairy tales, oral histories, and snatches of poetry whose deliberate awfulness amuses us even as it unsettles us. This sort of brilliant cognitive dissonance is a hallmark of Link's particular brand of fiction.

The story begins easily enough. Samantha and Claire are twin sisters, aged ten. Following their mother's death, their father has relocated them to Eight Chimneys, a typical Gothic mansion complete with exactly one hundred windows, three storeys, and a supposedly haunted forest. It is revealed that the girls' father has been studying the literary stylings of the house's previous occupant, Charles Cheatham Rash, who wrote 'three volumes of bad obscure poetry, and an even worse and more obscure novel'

(888). While their father works, the twins are cared for by the nameless babysitter, fourteen years old, who comes and goes as she pleases. Their favourite game is playing Dead ('When you're Dead ... you don't have to brush your teeth ...'; 'When you're Dead ... you live in a box and it's always dark, but you're not ever afraid.') (888). One day they discover the Specialist's hat hanging on a nail in the attic, apparently made by the poet Rash out of the fifty-two teeth of a range of exotic creatures as well as those of his own vanished wife. The Specialist's hat, we are told, looks like nothing, but it can sound like anything. The plot of the story itself follows a kind of dream logic that makes it difficult to précis; but its effects creep up on you, a sort of shivery, nerveless numbness, the mental equivalent of knocking your funny bone badly. Is it a love story? A ghost story? Does it end happily or not? Most readers would agree the story is fundamentally disquieting; but few, I think, could agree on *why*.

YOU CAN'T MAKE A *HOMMELETTE*...

While searching for a way to explain the curious effects of 'The Specialist's Hat', I found myself recalling 'Troubles with the Real', an essay written by the Marxist philosopher and cultural critic Slavoj Žižek, which I first encountered as a graduate student. The essay, a strange piece of Gothic-tinged criticism in its own right, discusses a monstrous figure first described by the psychoanalyst Jacques Lacan as the lamella or the *hommelette* (the 'man-omelet'), a membranous creature that apparently flies off the moment the foetus emerges. It is extra-flat, moving like an amoeba, capable of surviving any division, and, for all intents and purposes, immortal. 'Well!' exclaims Lacan, 'This is not very reassuring. But suppose it comes and envelopes your face while you are quietly asleep...' (197-98).

Suppose, indeed! What a horrifying thought! That element of horror was something Žižek picked up on in Lacan's account of the lamella, leading him to make the leap between the psychoanalytical concept (the lamella represented for Lacan the libido or the 'death drive') and the horror genre. For Žižek, the lamella — indivisible, indestructible, and immortal, an 'entity of pure surface ... first heard as a shrilling sound, and then [popping] up as a monstrously distorted body' — is *undead*, possessed not of a 'sublime spiritual immortality' but rather the 'obscene immortality' of a zombie. It is a creature which cannot die; it recomposes itself in the face of violence and clumsily staggers on. It is unstoppable, a representation of 'an uncanny excess of life'; it is the urge to persist beyond the natural cycle of generation and corruption. Žižek memorably compares the lamella to the face-hugger in Ridley Scott's *Alien*, an indestructible creature which multiplies when it is cut into pieces, and whose extra-flat body can suddenly fly up and envelop your face: 'In it,' he writes, 'pure evil animality overlaps with machinic blind insistence.'

So far, so terrifying — but what does it have to do with Kelly Link? In rereading 'The Specialist's Hat' for the umpteenth time, I noticed a striking similarity between the eponymous piece of clothing and Žižek's lamella:

> Hanging from a nail on the nursery chimney is a long black object. It looks lumpy and heavy, as if it were full of things. ... There are holes in the black thing, and it whistles mournfully as [the babysitter] spins it. 'The Specialist's hat,' she says.
> 'That doesn't look like a hat,' says Claire. 'It doesn't look like anything at all.' (893)

And then:

> Claire snatches the hat off the nail. 'I'm the Specialist!' she says, putting the hat on her head. It falls over her eyes, the floppy shapeless brim sewn with little asymmetrical buttons that flash and catch the moonlight like teeth. (893)

Is this not an eerily evocative description? The lumpy,

shapeless, toothy object which emits a strange sound and creeps over your face in order to seal it up? 'Yes,' you might cry, 'but so what? What does it *mean*?' Or better yet: 'Why does it frighten me?'

Here we might return to that classic ghost story I mentioned at the beginning of the essay: 'Oh, Whistle and I'll Come to You, My Lad' by M. R. James, a tale with a rather similar uncanny presence. When Professor Parkins arrives for an off-season visit at a seaside hotel, he wanders into the vicinity of a ruined Templars church where he discovers an ancient whistle engraved with the words QUIS EST ISTE QUI VENIT (Who is this who is coming?). The sound of the whistle fascinates Parkins, but as he sleeps he is haunted by a terrifying vision of a long stretch of shore, absent of any distinguishing features except a man, fleeing:

> So far no cause whatever for the fear of the runner had been shown; but now there began to be seen, far up the shore, a little flicker of something light-coloured moving to and fro with great swiftness and irregularity. Rapidly growing larger, it, too, declared itself as a figure in pale, fluttering draperies, ill-defined. There was something about its motion which made Parkins very unwilling to see it at close quarters. It would stop, raise arms, bow itself toward the sand, then run stooping across the beach to the water-edge and back again; and then, rising upright, once more continue its course forward at a speed that was startling and terrifying. (20)

The subsequent night, Professor Parkins discovers the entity has invaded his room, taking up residence in the empty second bed, a rustling and shaking thing to be described later as 'a horrible, an intensely horrible, face of crumpled linen' (26). In a fit of panic, Parkins dashes for the whistle which he has left by the window:

> This was, as it turned out, the worst thing he could have done, because the personage in the empty bed, with a sudden smooth

motion, slipped from the bed and took up a position, with outspread arms, between the two beds, and in front of the door. Parkins watched it in a horrid perplexity. Somehow, the idea of getting past it and escaping through the door was intolerable to him; he could not have borne — he didn't know why — to touch it; and as for its touching him, he would sooner dash himself through the window than have that happen. (26)

For all intents and purposes, the monstrous apparition of James's story possesses the very same qualities as the Specialist's hat: it is formless and flat, nothing more than crumpled linen and yet somehow indestructible, indescribable and intensely horrible. Like the lamella, it emits a strange noise, and it can move at a terrifying speed. It unsettles because its lack of form speaks to its monstrous immortality; how would you destroy such an entity? Is it even possible? What *is* it? If we return to the inscription on the whistle, we discover our question is only repeated back to us: *Quis est*? Who is this?

This is precisely the question that Link returns to in the chilling conclusion of 'The Specialist's Hat.' Claire and Samantha have worn the Specialist's hat, they have allowed themselves to enter a strange stasis, somewhere between the Death of their childhood game and real annihilation. '*He'll* be coming soon,' the babysitter tells them. 'It will be coming soon' (894). But who is the Specialist? There are only vague hints and suggestions.

> *Who's there?*
> *Just air.* (894)

No one is there. Nothing is there. Or rather nothingness is there. Death.

And then the front door opens. Samantha and Claire huddle together as they listen to someone creeping up the stairs. 'Be quiet,' the babysitter commands them. 'It's the Specialist.' And then we hear him ourselves:

'Claire, Samantha, Samantha Claire.' The Specialist's voice is blurry and wet. It sounds like their father's voice, but that's because the hat can imitate any noise, any voice. 'Are you still awake?' (894)

Is it their father who has come for them? Or is it, as the babysitter suggests, the Specialist? And is *this* what we find terrifying in the story: the disappearance of the father, his replacement by a simulacrum, almost identical, someone who pretends to love them but who is fundamentally a stranger? *Quis est?* Perhaps this is *part* of the terror, but it isn't everything. What leaves us most disturbed, I think, is not their father's transformation into the Specialist but rather their own transformation, facilitated by their interaction with the Specialist's hat — the lamella. And in fact it is the lamella that they themselves seem to become. Think about it. They gain the ability to move strangely, to vanish up the chimney and fly, if they want to, from the bed; they are trapped in a kind of pre-sexual stasis between ten and eleven; they are indivisible:

Last year they were learning fractions in school, when her mother died. Fractions remind Samantha of herds of wild horses, piebalds and pintos and palominos. There are so many of them, and they are, well, fractious and unruly. (894)

Their mother's death has left them in this state, but they have also chosen it; as a game, as an escape, as a way of liberating themselves from the need to grow up. Like the zombie, the alien, and the spectral presence, they have taken upon themselves an obscene form of immortality; they are *undead*.

...WITHOUT BREAKING A FEW EGGS

But what then is 'The Specialist's Hat' *about*? At one level, this is a story invested with enough sexual imagery to make it any psychoanalyst's (wet?) dream. We begin with Samantha and Claire, two pre-pubescent girls who lose their mother, only to find that their widower father has recently met a woman in the woods. We learn that the woman is a distant relation of Rash; we know by this point that Rash had a pretty wife who met another man 'who wanted to go with her' (889). When Rash's wife finally agreed, her husband found out and tricked her into drinking the blood of a snake:

> And in about six months snakes created in her and they got between the meat and the skin. And they say you could just see them running up and down her legs. They say she was just hollow to the top of her body, and it kept on like that till she died. (889)

This is the first explanation we hear of what sex might mean in the context of the story: snakes, hollowness, and eventually death. The image of the snake reoccurs throughout the story. One of Rash's poems tells how he met a woman in the wood, and 'her lips were two red snakes' (890). The Specialist's hat makes a noise like a snake. Most importantly, when the girls' father comes stumbling into the bedroom, he claims, 'I think I've been bitten by something. I think I've been bitten by a goddamn snake' (894). The sense of this image is clear: the snake is a symbol of consuming sexuality, a creature that hollows you out, and eventually kills you. Only the twins, who escape as ghosts through the chimney, remain untouched.

So what might Žižek say about this? Recall that the lamella is itself a representation of the libido in Lacanian theory. He describes it as the irrepressible sexual urge, the death drive, the drive for 'an uncanny excess of life.' It is also something thrown off from the foetus, amoeba-like, the *thing without any sex of its own*. It is pre-sexual. The symbolic resonance of the snake as a representation of the lamella is obvious. What haunts Samantha and Claire is the fear that their father has become fundamentally different because of his libido, somehow alien to them; he has vanished into the woods to meet his lover, and he has been bitten by the snake; it will kill him — or worse yet, it will *change* him.

But the real anxiety, I think, is not simply what the snake has done to their father, but what it will do to *them*. Sexual women become dead women in this story: Rash's wife, their own mother. And so they must find a way to stop themselves from growing older, from falling into the inevitable trap of puberty. 'Samantha doesn't care for boys that much,' the story reminds us.

> She likes numbers. Take the number 8 for instance, which can be more than one thing at once. Looked at one way, 8 looks like a bent woman with curvy hair. But if you lay it down on its side, it looks like a snake curled with its tail in its mouth. This is sort of like the difference between being Dead and being dead. (894)

For Samantha, the image of the number 8 oscillates between the form of the bent woman, the sexual woman, and the snake devouring itself. Becoming a sexualized woman is like being Dead: it is liberating, the Dead fear nothing, the Dead can move as they will. But the snake also symbolises true death or annihilation: 'The morning comes not, no, never, no more' (892). When the twins put on the Specialist's hat — the ultimate vagina *dentata* — they gain control of their sexuality, or rather, they gain the power to annul their own sexuality, to control it. The Specialist's hat, then, is both a sign of what haunts them and the mechanism by which they learn to escape it.

But the horror of the lamella extends beyond a purely sexualised reading of the story. It is truly disturbing, Žižek might say, because it represents the intersection between the imaginary and the Real; it reveals the Real in its most terrifying dimension as the primordial abyss which dissolves all identities and swallows everything. This concept of the Real will be familiar to readers of weird fiction. It is represented in a range of literary guises from Poe's maelstrom to the horror at the end of Joseph Conrad's *Heart of Darkness* to Lovecraft's elder god Cthulhu, a creature who presents such a dangerous vision of the universe that he cannot be seen without causing madness:

> The most merciful thing in the world, I think, is the inability of the human mind to correlate all its contents. We live on a placid island of ignorance in the midst of black seas of infinity, and it was not meant that we should voyage far. The sciences, each straining in its own direction, have hitherto harmed us little; but some day the piecing together of dissociated knowledge will open up such terrifying vistas of reality, and of our frightful position therein, that we shall either go mad from the revelation or flee from the deadly light into the peace and safety of a new dark age. (139)

The critic Benjamin Noys identifies in Žižek's critical writing a true Gothic sensibility. For Lacan, the Real is inscribed into the notion of human sexuality, but for Žižek, the kernel of reality is horror, the horror of the Real — an encounter with the universe as it really is, stripped of imaginative protection and representation.

'The Specialist's Hat' terrifies us in much the same way that Lovecraft terrifies us: it hints at an encounter with something which is beyond the realm of our experience — death — and yet which is simultaneously so deeply embedded in our own nature that it is *always already there*. Beneath the awfulness of Rash's obscure poetry is an insight we recognise as fundamentally true: we are dying, we have always been dying, and sex, which seems to promise immortality, is not a way out of that trap, but rather a way further into it. Sex is the disappearance of the self, just as death is; there is no immortality, there is only the restless seeking after it, the repetition of the journey into the woods, the bite of the snake, and the hollowing out of the body as skin pulls away from meat, as you grow accustomed to slowness, as your eyes sink in, your flesh decays....

This repetition, this annihilation, this image of the future is what terrifies us — because we know it is true. The twins embrace another kind of formlessness — Death — as a way to ward off or sublimate the vision of natural death they witnessed when their mother passed away. The ambiguity of the ending comes not in the identity of the father — whether he has turned into the Specialist — or indeed in whether something awful has happened to the twins. Rather it comes in the irresolution of the twins' stasis: like Peter Pan, will they choose Death forever? Or will they accept life with all its dangers, its delusions, and its ultimate dissolution?

SURVIVAL STRATEGIES

The story 'Survival Strategies' originally appeared in *Black Static*, Issue 58 (2017). It was reprinted in *Best New Horror* 29, ed. Stephen Jones (PS Publishing, 2018) and *The Year's Best Fantasy and Dark Horror* 9, ed. Paula Guran (Prime, 2018).

Barron St John must have been nearing his seventies by that point. The pictures I'd copied from magazine covers and newspapers charted his rise from a rake-thin tower of a man, nearly six-three, clad in a badly fitting white wool jacket with a thick crop of black hair cut like a bowl around his ears to his older self: hair grey but still as thick as it had ever been, fine laugh lines etching the curve of that grinning, maniac mouth. In his heyday people had taken to calling him the King of Horror, a real scaremeister — that term always made me laugh — but the man I saw in those later pictures had the look of a grandfather, which I suppose he was, one who could spin a yarn, sure, but not the kid who'd posed with a shotgun for his university paper under the headline 'Vote dammit!'

My university had given me a small grant for my research project into St John's career. I had planned to stay in Hotel 31, the cheapest place Luca and I had agreed we could afford. He had wanted me in midtown so I could walk most places. He was a worrier, had never been to New York and the idea of me riding the subway right then made him uneasy.

'It'll be fine,' I told him, 'nothing will happen. It isn't like that anymore. It hasn't been since the '90s.' We both knew that wasn't exactly true. The situation was different now, but scarier in other ways. There were journalists being stopped at the borders, asked invasive questions. Not everyone was allowed in. And Luca, for all his woolly sweetness and soft English manners, had a serious stubborn streak. He was protective, I knew, and didn't like the idea of me traveling on my own, not after I'd reacted so badly to the procedure, and certainly not 'abroad' as he called it in that charmingly old-fashioned way of his.

But 'abroad' was what I had wanted. Even if it wasn't home for me, which lay four-hundred miles north across the border in Toronto where my sister lived, New York still felt more familiar than the still-drizzly streets of London in the summer. Besides, I suppose there was a part of me that wanted to see how bad things had got.

And St John was a new obsession of mine, one I'd taken up in my recovery. Luca had been reading his pulpy-looking paperbacks for years, but I'd never touched them. They were too scary, I'd thought, too low brow. I remembered the garish paperbacks though, the ones that showed off his last name in huge embossed letters. They'd been ubiquitous when I was a kid. Each had a plain black cover with a silhouette cutaway so you had to turn the page to get the full effect. *Rosie* was the first I ever saw, his debut, the starting point for his surprising upward trajectory. It featured a small New Hampshire town — eerily similar to the one where I'd grown up, what had once been a small farming community until the petroleum processing plants transformed it. The town was engulfed in a crackling lightning storm. *Gory and horrifying*, read the cover, *you can't put it down!!!*

St John didn't live in New York, but his former editor did: Lily Argo.

I'd found her e-mail address online. Like St John she must have been in her seventies but was still working freelance. There were no pictures. The best I could find was a black and white shot of her and St John at the signing of his fourth book, *What Is Mine*, the last they worked on together. Lily Argo was an inch or two taller than St John, glorious, an Allison Janney look-alike, which meant the two of them towered over the line of moist-lipped teenage girls who were clustered around the table. That was back in '79.

When I first approached one of my friends — an anthology editor named Dylan Bone (real name or not, I never knew) — about the possibility of an article on the publication of *Rosie*, he told me Argo had died. Dylan had even written up her obituary for *Locus* – but in retrospect he couldn't remember how he'd first found out. She'd been one of the few female editors at Doubleday back then, mostly due to her lucky discovery of St John. When I mentioned I'd been in contact with her, that she'd agreed to meet me, Dylan had stared at me thoughtfully.

'Just be careful,' he said.

'About what?'

He'd just waved his hand. 'You know,' he said before lurching off to the bar to fetch another round.

I didn't have any problems with the border guards. The customs line was tense, but I'd always had that feeling whenever I entered the States. Once I'd swallowed two painkillers before a flight back to London and the random swipe they'd done on my hands had registered a false positive for explosives or drugs. I'd been taken to a small backroom where a dark-haired woman in a uniform demanded to know why I had been in the country. I kept apologizing, I don't know why. She had to search me by hand and the process was brusque and businesslike. She asked me to remove my bra. Then someone else came in, a heavy-set man with a broad forehead. He didn't look at me. Neither of them did. Afterward they let me go but ever since I'd been stopped for 'random' checks whenever I boarded a plane. This time though the guard took one look at me and waved me through. I must have looked harmless to him.

Hotel 31 was as old as the Overlook, mostly derelict with a walk-in elevator whose grill door you had to close yourself. The room was sparse, but by that point exhaustion had sunk into my skin. I called Luca to tell him I'd arrived and then collapsed under the thin covers.

All night I could hear animal sounds in the walls. The bodies of whatever moved beyond the peeling wallpaper hummed like batteries. Still, I slept. And in the morning I felt better than I had in weeks. Not mended, but stronger.

I was still in that dusky phase of grieving so that sometimes when I slept it felt I had fallen through a hole in the world. Each morning I woke up as a different person, discovered new wrinkles at the corner of my eyes, wires of thick, unrecognizable, grey hair. The doctor warned me of changes in my body, cramping, small clots of blood between my legs. I had expected my breasts to shrink but they'd only gotten larger. I read online the best thing to do was to bind them tightly with a snug towel and apply ice for ten minutes on, twenty minutes off. He hadn't told me how old I would feel after.

I had given myself three days to acclimatise to jetlag before I met up with Lily Argo.

In the mean time I'd arranged a visit to Doubleday, St John's first publisher. In the last thirty years Doubleday had joined with Dell and Bantam which in turn joined up with Random House. Size, they had thought, was the best way to survive an uncertain economic climate.

Two weeks ago, I'd contacted an editor at Random House in the hopes he might know if the company had kept some of the records from St John's days. But after the bag search and the metal detectors, when I was buzzed into the offices, a blonde receptionist told me my meeting had been postponed. She was young, slickly made up in that New York way with manicured fingers and perfect plucked eyebrows. I was wearing a dark blue cardigan which, seeing her, suddenly felt so English, so matronly I almost laughed.

So I waited in the reception for an hour, browsing the display copies of new books by Margaret Atwood and Chimamanda Ngozi Adichie. They too were slickly produced.

After a while I pulled out my beat-up copy of *Strangers and Friends*, a collection of short stories St John had published in gentlemen's magazines like *Cavalier* and *Penthouse* over the years. The book had never been one of St John's most popular, but I'd been thumbing my way through it slowly for weeks. On the flight I had started a story called 'The Survivalist' in which a doctor finds himself trapped alone in a bunker after a nuclear blast. He lives there for years, decades, devouring canned peaches and Spam until finally he comes to the end of his stashed supplies. He knows he doesn't have many options left. He can open up the door, risk contamination for a sight of the outside world — or he can continue to wait. The doctor stares at the door, wanting desperately to go out, but he can't bring himself to open it. The story ends as, driven half-mad with hunger, he begins to contemplate how long he could survive eating first the flesh of his legs, his thighs, how much he could withstand. He is a doctor after all, and he thinks it could be quite some time....

The story was gross, and it had all the macabre glee you would expect from a St John chiller. But I didn't feel scared by it. No, what upset me most was its sense of futility. The doctor had given up on hope. He wasn't waiting for rescue. He didn't believe anyone else in the world was alive. He was simply ... persisting. If he was the last man on earth, he wanted to last as long as possible. It was grotesque. Why didn't he open the door? That's what Luca would say when I tried to explain the plot him. But then Luca was the kind of man who *would* have opened the door. He couldn't see another way of living.

Another hour passed. Eventually the receptionist waved me over. Her manicured nails glinted dully in the light. 'I'm sorry, ma'am,' she said, 'but the records from those years haven't been maintained. I didn't even know we were the ones who published Barron St John.' She gave a little laugh.

I asked her what that meant for me.

'No one's free to meet you. We converted to digital years ago,' she said, barely sparing me a glance. 'Whatever we had, we dumped back then. Besides, who reads that trash anyway?'

After that I found myself at loose ends, so I called up a friend of mine, Benny Perry.

Benny and I had gone to grad school together at the University of Toronto, both of us doing doctorates in medieval literature in those early days after the financial crash when we still thought the market would recover enough to give us jobs. I'd kept at it, spinning my work on the scribal culture that produced Chaucer's *Canterbury Tales* into a postdoc in Oxford and then riding that into a full-time position in Publishing Studies of all things at a former polytechnic university. It wasn't glamorous, not like Oxford had been, but I liked the students, I liked my colleagues, and I liked the work itself: imagining how books moved through time and all the people who left their mark on them along the way.

Benny had taken another route. He'd always had a talent with photography and after he dropped out of the program he'd moved to New York and taken a job with *House & Garden* before it closed. It'd paid well enough that he'd stuck with photography, jumping from one magazine to another until he had enough of a portfolio to go freelance. He'd taken one of those famous pictures of Trump, the one where his face seems to be receding into the folds of flesh around his neck. In the past couple of months, I'd seen it on social media from time to time and reprinted in the papers.

'It's made things a bit hard for me,' Benny told me as we sat sipping margaritas in The Lantern's Keep, a classy place near Times Square where the cocktails cost four times what they would at home. There had been a teary week before Luca and I made our decision when I'd given up alcohol, and even after we changed our minds I still hadn't felt like touching the stuff. This was the first drink I'd had in eight months.

'How do you mean?'

'Well it's brought me lots of attention, sure, but not the good kind, you know? Trump supporters *hate* that picture. Trump does too, which is why it gets recycled so often.'

Benny's face looked strained and he fidgeted with his glass. He wasn't quite how I remembered him. Benny was always a big man, a cornfed, Iowa type whose Baptist parents had taught him to shun dancing and drink. When I'd met him at orientation, he'd been shy, a bit overwhelmed. But after those first awkward weeks he'd just thrown himself into everything. He had this irrepressible love of the new, and he'd taken to those things he'd missed out on most: booze, women — then men, dancing late into the night with this kind of unselfconscious clumsiness which made you want to join in.

He was much thinner now, that kind of thinness that didn't look healthy. 'I'm worried about Emmanuel,' he said, 'worried about ... well. Anyway. People can be absolute shits, can't they?'

I agreed that they could.

'But you're looking good,' Benny said, and I caught his eyes skimming over my breasts. Even though it didn't mean anything coming from him I still blushed and pulled at the cardigan. 'But not ... I don't know, maybe not entirely good?' he was going on. 'Hell. I don't know what I'm trying to say.'

I took his hand gently and told him not to worry about it.

As The Lantern's Keep started to fill up, eventually we wandered out into the street. It was hot and swampy, that kind of early August weather that makes you feel as if you've been wrapped in a damp blanket and beaten. We headed south toward the West Village by foot so I could see the sights. North was Central Park and Trump Towers, which were all basically off limits now. New York hadn't changed so much, not in terms of that strange and beautiful blend of architecture and anger, but there were bits that alarmed me. Like all the police cars had stickers listing the reward for information on cop-killers with a number you could call.

When I told Benny about the project I was working on, it turned out he'd read St John as a kid, which surprised me, given his background.

'What I remember about him was that my parents were reading him. They never read *anything* like that otherwise. Murder and cannibalism and demons and all that stuff. But *Faction of Fire*, you know, it was all about faith, wasn't it? In that book there was no getting around it: The Devil was real. And I suppose that's what my parents thought anyway. Good and evil weren't abstract concepts to them. There were good folk and there were bad folk. And it wasn't just that the bad folk made bad decisions. They were ... *bad*. It was something more fundamental. Badness worked through them. It was something tangible, real. And St John, well, his books were all about that, weren't they?'

Benny grinned at me and for a moment I could see his younger self peering out, that kid who'd never touched a drop of liquor in his life before I met him.

'How're your parents doing?' I asked him because that was the kind of thing we were supposed to ask one another now that we weren't kids anymore.

'Dad had a stroke two years ago,' Benny said with a shrug. 'I go back when I can to help her out. She's lonely, I know, but whenever I do go we just end up fighting.'

I didn't ask him about Emmanuel, about whether his parents knew. I figured probably they did. There were enough profiles floating around about Benny's photos so you could only avoid knowing if you really tried.

'How are you and Luca doing?'

'Good.'

'He didn't want to come with you?'

'Couldn't get away. You know how it is with these NGOs. Anytime he leaves he feels like he's letting people down.'

'It's good what he's doing,' Benny told me. 'We need more people like him right now.' After a moment he stretched, and I heard the joints in his shoulders pop. 'It must be hard writing horror stories now, you know? It seems like that's all we've got these days. I can't bear to watch the news anymore.'

I didn't sleep well that night. When I'd glanced at the papers, they were filled with stories about tensions escalating, something to do with the South China Sea islands and whether the U.S. was being too aggressive. John McCain was trying to dial things back, but you could tell he was getting tired of it. His eyes looked sharp and a little bit scared.

I'd had panic attacks all throughout the October leading up to the election. There'd been Brexit, of course, our own particular mess. At a conference last summer an American colleague had told me, 'what we're seeing is radical politics. People stopped believing that they mattered to the system — but all that's different now. It's exciting, isn't it? Anything could happen.' Trump had seemed funny back then, dangerous but still avoidable. They called it all a horror show but you could tell there was fascination underneath it all. How close could we come to disaster? But Hillary was ahead in the polls. Some of the Republicans were denouncing Trump, trying to put a little distance between themselves for when the eventual shellacking came on November 8th.

But it didn't come. For weeks after, all throughout the Christmas break, whenever I heard Trump's name it was as if there was a loud gong echoing in my head. My feed was filled with anguish, betrayal, heartbreak. But I had seen all that already. I felt immured, resilient — and besides I still didn't believe, not really, that it would happen. Then eventually the cold hard truth settled in when I watched the inauguration with Luca. As Trump walked to the podium, I burst out laughing, I don't know why, the sheer cognitive dissonance of the whole thing. I felt hysterical. My palms were sweating.

Afterward I learned St John had written a novel about something similar, *Answering the King*, about a madman who cheats his way to becoming the president of the United States. Eventually it comes down to a fifteen-year-old girl tormented with visions of the past and the future to stop him. The question at the heart of it is: if you could go back in time to stop Hitler, would you? They had made a movie about it with Steve Buscemi. I don't remember who played the girl, only how wide her eyes were, how she captured that world-weariness so well for someone so young. She was a Cassandra. No one would listen to her.

That was the night when the whole thing with Luca happened. Normally we were very careful. I hadn't been in my job for very long, and he'd just moved across the country to live with me. We had talked about having kids one day but ... we weren't careful enough. Disaster crept in the way it always does.

I called Argo the next day. It was the first time I'd spoken to her and her voice was thin and cagey with a flat, Ohio accent. It sounded as if it were coming from much further away than the Upper East Side.

It felt strange to be listening to her voice and I thought about what Dylan Bone had told me. I'd read the obituary in fact, half as a joke and half because I knew Dylan didn't make mistakes very often. He'd cut his teeth in the eighties horror boom and still made most of his money by convincing writers like St John and Clive Barker to give him new material. It might sound mercenary, but it isn't, not really: Bone was a believer, a horror fanatic. He loved the stuff and even when the market dropped out of it in the nineties he had kept at it, putting out anthology after anthology with cheesy, hand-drawn skeletons or zombified hands reaching out of the grave. Argo had been part of that, someone who'd *made* the genre in its heyday.

On the phone Argo was polite and she agreed to meet me for lunch the next day at a cafe. 'It'll have to be close to my apartment,' she told me, 'I can't move very well now.'

I told her I understood and could meet her wherever she wanted.

'What's this about then? Really?' Her tone wasn't querulous but wondering. 'You know I wrote a chapter about working with St John for some anthology twenty years ago, *Devilish Discussions* or something like that.

I hesitated because I didn't really have an answer. Yes, I knew the story about how she'd been sent St John's first manuscript by mistake. It had been meant to go to her boss, but he'd been on vacation. She'd liked it but her boss wouldn't touch it, and she didn't have enough support inside Doubleday to push it through, not then, a low-level assistant. But they'd kept in touch, writing letters when the mood took one or the other. Then when *Rosie* had come along it had been 'a day of glory' — so she called it.

I gave her the answer I gave most of my colleagues. St John had changed the genre, really changed it. For one brief moment horror hadn't been the red-haired stepchild of fiction. Horror had been *king*. And I wanted to know how that had happened. Part of my answer was true. I'd always been fascinated by the way books were made, the countless decisions that went into them. But if I was really honest it was simply because I'd become a fan, a real fan — maybe not Dylan Bone level — but my admiration for St John was genuine.

It was more than that though. The real reason was one I couldn't quite put my finger on, but it had something to do with stories of chance — which St John's certainly was. And that underneath every story is a pivotal moment when things changed. I wanted to know what that looked like. I needed to know if Argo had understood when that manuscript crossed her desk what it would mean, if she'd felt a chill when he opened the envelope. Like someone had walked on her grave.

That afternoon Benny took me out to the Cloisters for old time's sake, and it was beautiful, just like he'd promised it would be. The place was a mishmash of architecture taken from a series of medieval abbeys in France, Catalonia, and Occitania, simultaneously peaceful and surreal, liminal, a sliver of another world transplanted into New York.

'I thought you'd like it,' Benny told me. We were staring at a tree that had been shaped to fit one of the alcoves in the garden. Its branches curved unnaturally like a menorah to fill the space. I couldn't help but wonder how it had been manipulated, what sort of subtle violence had pressurized the wood to assume the shape it had.

'I do,' I told him, shivering despite the mid-day heat.

'So, tomorrow. The editor, what's her name again?' He snapped his fingers. 'Argo, right? Lily Argo. You're going to interview her. What about St John then? Any chance you'll get to speak to him?'

I didn't think so. St John lived in New Hampshire, and I had no idea what kind of relationship the two of them still had. If they kept in touch. If Argo would even like me.

'Of course she will. You're — well, you're the *makeles quene*, aren't you?' He smiled. 'You are without blot.'

'Someone back home said she was dead,' I told him uneasily. I still didn't like that part of the story. Why would Dylan have thought that?

'Huh,' Benny said. 'It sounds like the beginning of a ghost story, doesn't it? Like she'll bestow her wisdom on you, settle her unfinished business, and vanish into the night.'

'It sounds exactly like that.'

'But maybe you're lucky, not seeing St John.'

I asked him what he meant.

'You know. He's bound to be pretty weird, isn't he? I mean he's been writing that stuff for more than forty years now. You can't keep that close to the darkness without some of it sticking to you.'

It wasn't the first time I'd heard something like this before. I was used to getting it myself, sometimes at the university. But the horror writers I'd met were among the most well-adjusted people I knew, certainly they were much calmer than the other writers I tended to deal with. Some people said it was because there wasn't much money in horror writing these days. But I thought it was something else: writers were good at channeling their anxieties into something productive. We all have those nasty thoughts, those worries that maybe we don't love our partners as much as we should, or maybe they don't love us. Fears that maybe something awful will happen tomorrow. The phone will ring and it will be the police. An accident somewhere. Or a fight escalated, a button pushed.

'When I studied the Middle Ages,' I told him, 'it always seemed like it must have been so difficult for those people. I mean, the Black Death wiped out 40% of the population. Imagine whole villages lost, your family — everyone you've ever met — wiped out.'

'I know,' he said, 'I just couldn't take living like that. I'd, I dunno. I'd go crazy, I guess.'

I wondered if he really would go crazy. Or if he was going crazy right now, waiting for that call about Emmanuel. Waiting for Trump to finally get around to signing a new executive order. I had always liked Benny because he had a sense of outrage, a keen abhorrence of injustice. I knew he had marched in those early protests, and knew that he wasn't marching anymore. He didn't want to draw attention to himself. Benny was strong but he was adaptable. He was finding ways to survive, to keep making his art — but doing it so it didn't hurt Emmanuel.

Luca was the same way. Most nights he didn't come home until close to midnight. There was always more he felt he could be doing. For a while I'd felt really proud of him. And then when things got bad, I'd just felt resentful, angry at him for spending so much time saving other people when what I really wanted was for him to save me.

In the gift shop I chose a postcard for him, a picture of the Flemish tapestry called *The Hunt for the Unicorn*. It showed five young men in aristocratic clothing with their spears and their dogs. If it weren't for the title you wouldn't have been able to tell what they were doing there. I wanted to choose one with the unicorn, but all of them looked too violent or depressing. Something about the unicorn in captivity, collared, in a fence that can barely hold her, reminded me of *Answering the King*, and how the girl had been taken to prison after she shot the president. There had been a coda at the end of the novel, the little girl twenty years later, grown up, in solitary confinement. They had thought she had gone mad because she wouldn't stop hurting herself.

But St John showed the real reason. The girl had had another vision, one worse than what she'd stopped all those years ago. But this time there was nothing she could do about it.

I couldn't get hold of Luca that night. He wasn't answering his e-mail and when I tried him at home — and then at work — the phone just rang and rang. It wasn't that unusual. Sometimes there were emergencies, and Luca would become so totally absorbed in them he would forget everything else.

There were emergencies like that, I knew, one every few days it seemed. So eventually I left a message saying I loved him. I tried the TV but got nothing except static. Eventually I settled down to read. It was another story from *Strangers and Friends* but this one was about a haunted house called 'Question the Foundations.' It was a twist on the trope: the houses weren't haunted by people so much as the people by houses. In St John's world each person had a tiny space within them, an impression of the place where they had been born. And it remained there, like a scar, or a memory. And everyone else could see it too, who you were and where you came from. Except there was this young boy who didn't have a place like that. He had nothing. He had come from nowhere. And because he had nothing, he scared people.

I put the book down, confused and unsure of myself. The story bothered me but I didn't know why. It was different from the others, softer, sadder. There was no real horror in the story. It had been about loneliness. How it felt to be hollow, an outsider. Rootless.

Maybe it was just those constellations of images, emptiness and violence. Luca had told me a story once about how his family used to keep chickens. He had lived in the middle of a wood. One day a fox broke into the henhouse and tore open all the chickens. He'd found their bodies, or what was left of them, the next morning. Inside their bodies he had found strings of growing eggs, like pearls.

After he told me that, I couldn't sleep, and it was the same feeling now. I didn't have any regrets. Luca and I had talked, and he had left the decision to me. There had been no pressure, none from him anyway. But I'd been watching the news. And when the first bomb exploded in Paddington Station it had been like a warning sign. Not now. It wasn't safe. Things would settle down soon, they had to. And then we could try again.

I put the book down and touched my stomach gently, tentatively. Beneath my fingers all I could feel was my own thick flesh.

Three times I passed the cafe before I finally had the courage to meet Lily Argo. I could see her — at least I thought it was her — sitting in the courtyard with her walker folded up beside her. She had long white hair and a red-and-grey printed dress with long sleeves. I knew her because of how tall she was, even a little stooped over. She still had at least six inches on me.

'Ms. Argo?' I asked her and she nodded politely while I pulled up a seat.

'So you're the one who's come asking about Barron St John.'

'That's right.' I tentatively launched into my pitch: an article on St John's early publication history, documenting her involvement in acquiring and editing his first title. She stopped me with a wave of her hand.

'Sure, honey,' she said with a wide, generous smile, 'you don't need to go on like that. I'm happy to talk about those days, though I confess they seem a while ago now. You know I got that manuscript by accident, don't you?'

I nodded, and she seemed relieved.

'Good, so we're not starting from scratch. What you want is the story, I take it, of how Bear — that's what I always called him — and I got along in those early days? Where the horror came from?' I nodded again and took out my phone but she eyed it warily. 'I'll tell it as best I can and you can make of it whatever you will — but no recordings, okay? You can listen and you can write down what you get from it, but you only get to hear it once.'

What was I supposed to say? Already I could feel a kind of strange buzz around her, the magnetic pull of her charisma. I had wanted her story and here she was, ready to give it to me.

'I was pretty young in those days,' she began, 'when I first started working for Doubleday. I'd grown up in Ohio which I never liked very much in part because it didn't seem like I was much use to my parents. I was a reader, even then, but they had wanted me to go to one of the nursing schools, but I knew I'd never be happy with something like that, taking care of people all the time. So when I was seventeen I ran off to New York City.

'Publishing was still very much a gentleman's sport back then and if you were a woman you were either someone's secretary or you were publishing feminist pamphlets and burning your bra. I was the former.' She paused and took a delicate sip from her Coke. Her lipstick remained unsmudged though it left a trace of red on her straw. 'Most of us at the time wanted to be writers. I suppose I did as much as anyone, and so we'd spend our days editing, and we'd spend our nights writing. What was funny was that we knew all the people we were sending our drivel to, we'd met them at luncheons or for after-hours drinks. I was embarrassed. I was a good editor, and *because* I was a good editor I knew I wasn't a very good writer. I thought, how on earth will these men take me seriously if they see what I'm coming up with?

'So I did what most women did at the time, or anyone who wasn't Daphne du Maurier anyway, and I made up a name. Mine was Victor Wolf, which today seems so damned fake I don't know why no one thought anything of it. Or maybe they did but they just didn't care. Anyway I may have been writing garbage, but eventually the garbage got better and I started getting some of it published. It was what they called Kooks and Spooks stuff, I suppose, sort of crime fiction but with some other bits thrown in, monsters, sometimes, and ghosts. Possession — or Russian spies using hypnosis to control young American teenagers, that sort of thing. There was a real taste for that sort of thing back then. By the early seventies the papers were going crazy, telling us the irrationalism of our reading was helping the Commies and we had to get back to old-fashioned, American literature. But *Rosemary's Baby* was an absolute hit, and then there was *The Exorcist*, and people just wanted more of it.

'That was when Bear's first manuscript came across my desk. The two of us call it an accident but it wasn't that, not really. See, I was used to reading submissions for Donnie Rogers and when I finished Bear's first one I knew there was magic in it, raw, maybe, but magic nonetheless. And I knew Donnie was slated for laparoscopic gallbladder surgery. He was going to be off for at least a week recovering. That was when I tried to pitch the manuscript.

'Of course, I got laughed out of the offices. No one took me seriously and when Donnie came back he heard what I'd done and he bawled me out in front of the whole crew. Jesus, he took a strip off one side of me and then the other. After that I didn't dare try anything like that for a good long while.

'Still, Bear had appreciated the support. He was poor as a church mouse and he and Mya had a second little one on the way. He tried me with this and that a couple of times, but it never really made it anywhere. I guess it was after a while of him sending me his stuff that I sent him one of mine. God, the nerve I had!' she chuckled, and I couldn't help but chuckle along with her. 'Well Bear wrote back and said it was pretty good, and I said it was better than pretty good, that *Playboy* had taken it. Bear had been trying to crack *Playboy* but hadn't managed it by that point.

'For six months Bear went silent after that, and I guess I thought maybe I'd offended him. Men don't like being shown up, not then, not now. That's why there's all the craziness there is today. Women are afraid of violence, but men? Men are afraid of humiliation. Humiliation to them is like dying over and over and over again. And speaking of humiliation, I had just about survived mine. Donnie Rogers had moved over to New American Libraries, and I was covering for him while they looked for a replacement. That was when the next manuscript crossed my desk.'

'That was *Rosie*?' I asked her.

'Indeed it was, though it was called *Revenge of the Stars* at the time which was a godawful title, I have to say.'

'And this time it stuck?'

'Not right away it didn't. The ending was clunky. It had Rosie transforming into this giant radioactive slug thing and devouring the town that way. Pure St John, you know. He always loved the EC Comics stuff. People want to say he's got literary chops, and sure he does, but a part of him is pure pulp and is perfectly content to stay that way, thank you very much.'

'So what happened?' I wanted to know.

'Oh, that's the easy bit. Some good luck, I suppose. Ira Levin was big, and Bear's book was enough like that for me to pull together an advance for him. Small, you know. The real success came later with the paperback sales, and that wasn't me, not exactly. But I suppose if what you're after is who found Barron St John then it's me as much as it was anyone.'

She paused there to take another long drag of her Coke. While she'd been talking, she seemed so animated, so full of vigor, but as the seconds stretched on I could see how old she was now, how time had etched fine lines around her lips. Her wrists were thin and frail, the skin bunching and slack at the same time.

She moved then, pulled up a black leather handbag and began to dig around in it. Eventually she came up with a Christmas card. 'Look at that,' she said, her eyes sharp. The paper was old and creased in several places. When I opened it there I found a simple handwritten note. *To Lilian*, it said, *a real wolf in sheep's clothing. We owe you so much. Love, Bear and Mya St John.*

Lily was smiling slightly as she showed it to me, smiling and watching to see my reaction. I tried to smile back but there was a part of me that felt disappointed. Most of the story was what she had published in that chapter. Little of it really surprised me. It felt rehearsed, the way you keep old memories by telling yourself the story behind them again and again. Whatever I was looking for, it wasn't there.

I was getting restless, and it seemed like she was finished when she cocked her head to the side. 'That's not what you wanted to hear, was it?'

I tried to tell her it was great, wonderful stuff. It would certainly make it into the article.

'Sure it will,' she said, 'but you didn't need any of it. Certainly you didn't need to fly over here from England just to get this story, did you? I could've told you that over the phone. You didn't need to come.'

I shrugged.

'What you wanted was him, wasn't it? You wanted Bear.'

'Maybe,' I told her wearily. The heat was starting to get to me, making me a touch queasy.

'It isn't easy, you know,' she said, 'to try to tell your story when the best parts are about someone else.' She sighed. 'You know, I had to give up writing once I found St John. It wasn't like it had been before. We were so busy all the time. St John could write like a madman, he was *fast*. There was always another book. And then things got tricky with the contracts. You must know about this?'

I did. Everyone did. St John had left Doubleday after a series of well-publicized contract disputes. Doubleday had been keeping most of the profits on the paperback sales, and he felt he deserved a bigger cut. Doubleday wouldn't budge and eventually he left.

'There wasn't much I could do for him. They wouldn't give him a better deal and they wouldn't listen when I told them how serious he was about leaving. When he finally did switch publishers all those men at the top said it was *my* fault. I got parked for a while editing books on what types of music you can play to help your plants grow, that sort of kooky trash. After a year or so they fired me.'

I fiddled with my own straw, unsure how to react to any of this.

'Bear didn't take me with him, see. I told him not to. I told him I had enough status in the company — but I was wrong. When you're on top you always think you're going to stay there forever, that there aren't sharks circling beneath. But I guess Barron knew about those sharks. The one thing he knew about was the sharks. He could be one himself when he needed to.'

'You didn't want to go back to writing?'

'Nah, I felt I'd spent my chance by that point. I think I had one lucky break in me — and it went to St John. There wasn't going to be another. I got by after that. I moved over to another house for a little while and convinced St John to come do a book for us. But by that point things were different. He was a superstar and I felt spent. I had had enough of horror. It was the eighties. Despite everything it still felt as if the world was falling apart. There was the banking crisis, the AIDS epidemic. The people weren't reading the news though. They were reading Bear.

'I did write one more story though. I tried to sell it myself, but no one would buy it. Victor Wolf had been forgotten. Bear liked it though. And he knew I was in danger of losing my mortgage. So he sent it out for me, under his name. When it sold to the *New Yorker* — his first real literary sale though God knows he deserved others and got them eventually — he gave me the profits.' Her smile then was bitter. 'I was grateful, you know. At the time he said it was only fair. I had made his name after all. I should get the use of it whenever I wanted.

'And I was grateful at the time. I kept my brownstone, paid it off eventually. When he sold the collection, he gave me the whole advance. For a while I thought about going back to Ohio, but I still couldn't admit to my parents I hadn't been able to last in New York. So instead I stayed.'

She stared at me for a moment or two after that, and I could feel the cool ripple of sadness passing over me like a shadow.

'Someone told me you died,' I said, just to break the spell of her silence.

'Of the two of us, Barron was always the shark, you see?' she told me wryly, 'No, I didn't die. I just learned something he never figured out: how to stay alive when you stop moving.'

That evening I collected my things from Hotel 31.

Benny offered to drive me to the airport, but I told him he didn't need to do that. I could get a taxi. The university had given me a budget for that. When he said okay it sounded like there was relief in his voice, and I wondered if that meant Emmanuel was home. Or maybe it was just that he didn't want to get so close to the airport. There were regular protests still going on. People were angry about the deportations, but no one knew how to stop them.

'Did you get what you wanted from Lily Argo?' Benny asked me. 'She wasn't just a ghost?' I told him I hadn't really known what I wanted but I was certain, despite everything, I had met Lily Argo. But I was probably going to scrap the story. My Head of Department would be pissed but that was how these things went. Sometimes you thought you had something, and you didn't.

What she had told me felt too invasive to write about. What I had wanted, I realized, was not just her story but a glimpse of her secret self. I didn't have a right to it. And that's what had made me want it even more. Maybe we all have a secret self: some of us keep it chained in the basement of our minds while others like St John learn how to feed it.

'Well,' he said, 'it was good to see you anyway. Give my love to Luca. You tell him to take proper care of you.'

I promised I would.

While I waited for my flight to board, I watched the news. We were all watching the news. We couldn't help it. Tense security officers patrolled the hallways with machine guns at the ready, just in case. There were fewer travelers those days, fewer coming in, fewer getting out. But I felt a kind of solidarity with the others as our eyes were glued to the screens. We were liminal people moving from one reality to another. We were going home.

So we watched the footage of explosions in Yemen. Pleas from refugees who had found themselves trapped in abandoned tenements, living in filth. It was only when I saw the story about the bomb that had gone off on a train along the Victoria Line that I remembered Luca still hadn't called me back.

I was watching them pulling survivors out of the rubble and the blood gelled to ice in my veins. I couldn't move. It had happened then. It had happened. Time seemed to slow. Luca mostly worked from Cambridge, but the NGO had offices in London. He went there from time to time. When had I last heard from him? Who could I call to check? But by that point the attendant was calling me forward. I didn't move. She called me again and the people behind me began to murmur. I must have had a dazed expression on my face, a look they didn't like. The attendant called me a third time as an officer drew near. It was only then I was able to move. I showed them my passport and made my way down the ramp.

Inside the plane most of the seats were empty. The air was canned, stale tasting in my mouth. I wondered if I might have a panic attack but out on the runway I didn't dare check my phone again. The hostesses were murmuring to each other. I could tell they were twitchy. But already a strange calm was taking hold of me — a sense of icy horror. There was something inevitable about what was happening. There was nothing I could do to stop it. Whatever had happened had happened.

And this feeling? It wasn't the same as all those St John books I had read. There I could find purpose, structure — meaning in all the bad things that had happened. But outside there was only chaos. The unraveling of beautiful things into violence. It signified nothing.

As the plane taxied down the runway I settled back in my chair and tried to sleep.

SURVIVAL STRATEGIES FOR WEIRD TIMES

This commentary on the short story 'Survival Strategies' was published for the first time in *The Diseases of the Head: Essays at the Intersection of Speculative Philosophy and Speculative Horror* (Punctum Books). 277-314.

1. AUTOBIOGRAPHY

Art sends us information from another place.

— Timothy Morton, *Hyperobjects: Philosophy and Ecology after the End of the World* (2013)

The[1] short story 'Survival Strategies' — first published in *Black Static* Issue 58 (2017) and reprinted in the present volume — offers a semi-fictionalized account of a young academic on a research trip to New York to interview the editor of Barron St John, a bestselling author who came to prominence during the horror boom of the 1970s and 80s. Set against the backdrop of the new Trump administration, it uses autobiographical elements to blur the line between fiction and reality. In doing so, it asks, where do the boundaries between 'true horror' and speculative horror intersect? To what extent can our situatedness in the present moment become a source of the uncanny?

The autobiographical elements of story are important. In the summer of 2016 I began a research project to investigate the publishing history of Stephen King's *Carrie* by the hardback publisher Doubleday in 1974. At the time, I argued that the unexpected success of *Carrie* launched 'the Stephen King phenomenon'[2] and was one of several important books inspiring the marketing approach to horror paperbacks from the late seventies to the early nineties. As with the publication of any breakthrough novel, the penning of *Carrie* had taken on its own mythological status. In one of the autobiographical sections of his memoir and guide to the craft, *On Writing* (2000), King opens up about his difficulty in producing a first draft. He managed three single-spaced pages, which he crumpled up and threw away only to have them rescued by his wife, Tabitha.[3] The sense of a historical moment interested me — as I imagine it was intended to. I had recently completed a Ph.D. in medieval literature and was accustomed to working in the archives, aware of how much material had been lost over the centuries. Studying a contemporary novelist was innately appealing: it promised abundance where I had previously encountered dearth. But there was also an extra voyeuristic angle. Here was a writer I admired intensely whose life I might be able to approach in some way through my research. I wanted intimacy.

I was not entirely prepared for what I would find. I contacted Bill Thompson, King's first editor at Doubleday, through his editorial freelance website and arranged a meet-up in New York. But in conversation with several horror fans, authors and editors — both in the U.K. and in the U.S. — I was repeatedly told it would be impossible to meet Thompson because he had passed away years ago. Let me avoid all ambiguity here: as I found when I met him, Thompson was still very much in the land of the living. But my repeated encounter with claims of his apparent death began to evoke that creeping-under-the-skin sensation of the 'fantastic' — that moment identified by the Russian structuralist Tzvetan Todorov in which something apparently supernatural is encountered, creating a period of hesitation as different possibilities are suggested and discarded.[4] I did not know how to react. I had been in contact with Bill Thompson, had exchanged e-mails and agreed on a date for meeting, but all that contact had been on-line with no further way of verifying his identity. *I nearly reached the point of believing*. This is the formula Todorov presents to sum up the spirit of the fantastic: '[e]ither total faith or total incredulity would lead us beyond the fantastic: it is hesitation which sustains its life.'[5] I lingered in that period of hesitation. Bill Thompson was alive, of course he was alive, but the sense of the uncanny soaked into my perception of him. The trip came alive with the possibility of the real unreal.

2. THE REAL UNREAL

> The most merciful thing in the world, I think, is the inability of the human mind to correlate all its contents. We live on a placid island of ignorance in the midst of black seas of infinity, and it was not meant that we should voyage far. The sciences, each straining in its own direction, have hitherto harmed us little; but some day the piecing together of dissociated knowledge will open up such terrifying vistas of reality, and of our frightful position therein, that we shall either go mad from the revelation or flee from the deadly light into the peace and safety of a new dark age.
>
> —H.P. Lovecraft, *The Call of Cthulhu* (1928)[6]

It was the summer of 2016, and already my world had been destabilized. The Brexit vote had shaken U.K. politics, threatening my university which was heavily reliant on E.U. students and E.U. research funds. In New York, the American election was in full swing, already tilting toward Trump. 'Be careful,' I told friends, 'it could happen here.' No one took me seriously.

In a 1989 issue of *SF Eye*, Bruce Sterling described slipstream writing as 'a kind of writing which simply makes you feel very strange; the way that living in the twentieth century makes you feel, if you are a person of a certain sensibility.'[7] Slipstream writing drew heavily on the fantastic; as Sterling said:

[I]t is a contemporary kind of writing which has set its face against consensus reality. It is fantastic, surreal sometimes, speculative on occasion, but not rigorously so. It does not aim to provoke a 'sense of wonder' or to systematically extrapolate in the manner of classic science fiction.[8]

Where science fiction seemed coherent, the vanguard of a single dominant ideology, slipstream was postmodern, infused with a sense of ironic detachment that seemed to exemplify the natural response to conditions in Anglo-America. But twenty-five years on, how might we describe the contemporary sensibility? In 2016 I was post-postmodern though I had not fully realized it yet. Post-truth, if you like, or rather, pre-post-truth, which is not to say that I was living in a time of truth but rather that we had not recognized its loss. I was locked in a moment of hesitation.

As I write this now, I find Todorov's notion of the fantastic an imperfect vehicle to describe the feeling of that year. He imagines the moment of hesitation as fragile and difficult to sustain, liable to collapse either into 'total faith' or 'total incredulity'. In the years since I have attempted to grapple with this problem. If the twentieth century offered slipstream as its primary mode — ironic and playful — then increasingly it seems as if the twenty-first will be a far *weirder* age. Here, I draw upon the definition of weird fiction as first proposed by H.P. Lovecraft in his seminal work 'Supernatural Horror in Literature' (1927) as writing which exhibits a 'malign and particular suspension or defeat of [...] fixed laws of Nature.'[9] This mode, discussed by Jeff and Ann VanderMeer, China Miéville, and Roger Luckhurst, among others, to me, plausibly evokes the feeling of living in the twenty-first century: an age thus far characterized by political crises, fake news, and environmental catastrophe.[10] It is an age in which the unreal intrudes upon consensus reality, shattering it with often terrifying consequences.

Of the writing I have encountered on the subject, that of the speculative realist Timothy Morton has most resonated with me.

An intimate understanding of the weird infuses his discussion of hyperobjects, real things with discernible impacts which cannot be apprehended in their entirety, but which affect our understanding of what it means to exist. He cites global warming as one significant hyperobject: its effects are massively distributed, so much so that the object itself becomes difficult to grasp, seeming to disappear from our vision or to undulate in our minds and in reality. Morton describes our present moment as the age of asymmetry, a period of hypocrisy in which the ironic detachment characteristic of many postmodern writers is impossible because there is 'nowhere to stand outside of things altogether.'[11] Hyperobjects engulf us. However much we seek to escape them, we find there is no *away*.

This view finds eerie parallels with the primary processes of weird fiction. It evokes the brilliant ghost film *Ju-on: The Grudge*.[12] This was an early foray of mine into horror. I could hardly stand to watch it. The violence seemed senseless and unmotivated. A series of abstract images presented themselves, many of which still haunt me. A ghost clings to the body of a woman, invisible only when she enters a shower and discovers someone else's hand in her hair, as she begins to wash it. Likewise, another woman attempts to escape from the vengeful ghost by crawling into her bed — the psychological source of the greatest safety. But it is too late. She discovers the ghost is already inside, with her. No escape was possible from the ghost of *Ju-on* because no space, however personal, however intimate, was unavailable to it. Likewise, the weird is a profoundly intimate form of writing, designed to haunt, to project a trace of unreality onto the surface of the real. It creates ruptures, and in doing so, makes briefly visible what lies beneath. We encounter this as an intrusion in most cases, but if it is an intrusion, it is only an intrusion of *some other thing* upon our closed-off perception of the world. Those things were not summoned into being by our perception of them. They already existed, independent of our encounter with them. One of the primary functions of the weird is to remind us how little we see, and how the influence of those things we do not see can still be deadly.

This sensibility flowed into the text of 'Survival Strategies' by itself. I did not set out to write a story about Brexit and Trump but the sense of dislocation, the uncanniness of these hyperobjects, permeated multiple aspects of the story, conflating the painfully personal and the public, the story of myself and the story of the world in which I found myself living. To attempt to write about Stephen King as a researcher was to realize that there was no detached, objective position from which I could undertake my research. The story of King was the story of America in the late seventies, and that story is still the story of the present moment: one riven with violence and uncertainty, asymmetries in power, wild successes and also devastating failures. It felt profoundly uncomfortable, and it felt uncomfortable in a way that resonated with the experience of Brexit and Trump, the double punch. Taken together they suggested a sort of rising tide of — something. It was not clear to me exactly what. But whatever it was seemed inescapable. It was as if Brexit and Trump were simply 'a local manifestation of some vast entity' — Morton's hyperobject.[13] I could not separate myself from it, just as I could not return King to a distance where writing about him seemed easy. The real possibility of encountering King triggered a flight into fiction. The only way to write honestly about the experience was to write myself away from it.

3. FLIGHTS

> As the plane taxied down the runway I settled back in my chair and tried to sleep.
>
> —Helen Marshall, 'Survival Strategies'[14]

The narrative voice of 'Survival Strategies' is detached and yet the detachment marks a deep emotional engagement. The narrator floats through events, cynical at times, but only as a mask; cynicism deflects, but the narrator absorbs from a distance she seeks to maintain, only to find that no distance is possible. The world intrudes, sometimes violently. In the true fashion of the weird tale, her encounter with Lily Argo demonstrates that the world has *always* dangerously intruded, the world has always *already* dangerously intruded. There is no safe vantage point to observe without becoming immersed. In short, it feels like the end of the world.

Morton has something specific to say about this sense of the ending world in the twenty-first century. He calls into question the notion of *world*, labeling it an 'aesthetic effect based on a blurriness and aesthetic distance.'[15] I cannot help but agree. The act of writing 'Survival Strategies' was a simultaneous engagement with and flight from an increasingly inexplicable world. Its world was my world, but not my world — the *unheimlich* home, a home that does not allow one to feel at home. The act of writing was an attempt to create, through aesthetic engagement, a new world. Literally, the act of writing was, for me, an act of worldbuilding.

The process of worldbuilding lies at the heart of speculative fiction and yet it is an area with which I have always struggled, perhaps because my own style is improvisational and intuitive rather than clearly structured along conventional lines. But more than this I find weird fiction a natural fit, because I find the real world — the world as I experience it — to be incoherent and uncanny. It has no respect for genre. My project in writing is not to mask these inconsistencies but to draw them out and highlight their effect. But inconsistency is often considered the sign of poor worldbuilding or a failure of craft. A recent blogpost by the science fiction author Charlie Stross began to clarify my problems with the conventional approach to worldbuilding. Stross candidly discusses his rejection of most contemporary science fiction writing on the basis of flawed worldbuilding:

> The implicit construction of an artificial but plausible world is what distinguishes a work of science fiction from any other form of literature. It's an alternative type of underpinning to actually-existing reality, which is generally more substantial

(and less plausible — reality is under no compulsion to make sense).[16]

Artificial but plausible — this is a formulation I have since returned to many times in my attempt to grapple with what fiction is and what it should do. There is a tension at work in Stross's rejection of science fiction. He seems to seek plausibility from his reading, which in this case coincides with artificiality. This artifice is necessary because, as he says, reality is under no compulsion to make sense. Fiction provides sense. Fiction creates coherence. As a result, the kind of fiction Stross is after — the plausible — is a kind he recognizes as *more real than real*, one which is therefore inherently *unreal*. Stross's position exemplifies Morton's claims about the aesthetic effects of the notion of the world. Drawing on *Lord of the Rings* as a prime example, Morton alludes to the *Gesamtkunstwerk* (total work of art),[17] a creation in which, as Carl Maria von Weber said in 1816, 'partial contributions of the related and collaborating arts blend together, disappear, and, in disappearing, somehow form a new world.'[18] The *Gesamtkunstwerk* is the ideal science fiction story in Stross's formulation, one in which the writer has total control of all aspects. However, for Morton, the *Gesamtkunstwerk* is suspect because the act of worldbuilding extends beyond fiction into the Real, which he also sees as artificial, falsely presented as coherent when in fact it is utterly weird.

Writers of weird fiction do not have the same expectations as writers of science fiction. Their worlds exhibit inconsistency. In fact, the *sine qua non* of the weird writer is that gap in consistency: the extra stair at the bottom of the staircase that makes the reader stumble, the grit in the reader's eye, the living dead. Opposed to Stross's model of the plausibly constructed world is M. John Harrison, an important figure in New Wave science fiction who has also contributed to the rise of the New Weird. He says:

> Every moment of a science fiction story must represent the triumph of writing over worldbuilding.

> Worldbuilding is dull. Worldbuilding literalises the urge to invent. Worldbuilding gives an unnecessary permission for acts of writing (indeed, for acts of reading). Worldbuilding numbs the reader's ability to fulfil their part of the bargain, because it believes that it has to do everything around here if anything is going to get done.[19]

Harrison's sensibility speaks to me. His argument is subtle and contentious within the field. He describes the conventional view of worldbuilding as 'a bad idea about the world as much as it is a bad idea about fiction.'[20] He rejects the notion of the author-God and warns against readers who expect the world of the story to be anything other than a story. For Harrison the invented world has no outward substantive. It adheres only in language and in that sense it is purely an aesthetic effect. Stross would not, I think, disagree with this, but the difference between the two lies in the kind of immersion they are seeking. Harrison prefers fiction which acknowledges what it does as 'a shell game, a sham,'[21] yet his work is not post-modern in the framework we have been discussing. In fact, he rejects postmodernism with its three impossible claims:

> ...firstly that we can change the real world into a fully prosthetic environment without loss or effort; secondly that there are no facts, only competing stories about the world; and thirdly that it's possible to meaningfully write the words 'a world' outside the domains of imagination or metaphor, a solecism which allows us to feel safely distant from the consequences of our actions.[22]

Reading, according to Harrison, ought to be a ludic act. It offers the possibility of escape, but of a substantially different kind. Escape *into*, not *away from*. Here, escape should not be misread as escapism. Where Stross looks for sense, Harrison's work is profoundly unsettling. It presents fiction as a vehicle for non-sense — the unraveling of sense, the minute exposure of senselessness. Crucially, it seems to acknowledge that I may not always know what I mean when I write. Writing is not the attempt to translate coherence of thought from one mind to another. My mind is mischievous. I am not an author-God. There is a need for other sense-makers here.

In Lovecraft's weird tales an encounter with the real leaves three possibilities: death, madness, or flight. In 2016 I found myself struggling to find a new response. If I am honest, I did not find it within 'Survival Strategies.' The inspiration for the story arrived after a sleepless night following a viewing of *The Invitation* (2015),[23] a claustrophobic film about a man named Will attending a dinner party hosted by his ex-wife, Eden. Eden and her new husband have, it seems, subscribed to the beliefs of a nihilistic death cult. Before its brutal conclusion, the film shows Will's unease as he is continually encouraged to ignore his growing anxieties through the constant weight of social pressure: surely everything is fine, the film seems to say, and it would be rude to leave, wouldn't it? Will hesitates. He cannot decide how to process the telltale signs of danger he sees around himself. Only one character does, and it is her fate that kept me up that night. Early on in the evening, one of the guests, Claire, unsettled by a game of 'I Want' she is forced to play, makes her excuses and is followed out of the house by one of the other guests, David, whose looming presence throughout presages the bloodbath he will later initiate. We never find out what happens to Claire. Does David murder her off-screen, or does she manage to flee to safety, warned by the niggling feeling in the back of her mind that something is wrong? Her fate was important to me, and as the night advanced, I was left wondering: how effective was her strategy? What if our niggling sense of danger is too little, too late? What if we cannot run because what we are fleeing is waiting for us everywhere?

Morton asks another question: 'What is left if we aren't the world?' What if — like one of H.P. Lovecraft's hapless intellectuals — our sense of control dissipates as we come to recognize our insignificance in the face of much larger forces? Morton's answer is startling: 'Intimacy,' he writes, 'we have lost the world but gained a soul.'[2] If we are not obliterated, we are made more real by the encounter. The narrator of 'Survival Strategies' boards the aircraft despite the panic of an ill-described terrorist attack in London. She settles into her seat as the plane launches into the air. Perhaps her husband is dead. Perhaps everything she believed in has fallen apart. She cannot decide. She hesitates. She falls into sleep. The story had no answers for me then, but now I think that was part of the point in writing it. As a story it is not fully coherent. The metaphors do not perfectly unravel into clear meanings. But then a story cannot perfectly digest what it encounters.

The narrator sleeps, but she will wake, flying *into*, not *away from*. The world had ended before she ever left London. What is to come is a new kind of intimacy with the real. And wisdom, we can hope — and survival.

---

1. I would like to thank Nina Allan whose many conversations on the subject have informed my own developing approach to weird fiction, as well as Anglia Ruskin University, who funded my research. Thanks also go to Bill Thompson for his generous interview, Bob Jackson for providing copies of a number of crucial documents, and Bev Vincent for his support and guidance on all things King-related. Many of the threads discussed in this commentary relate to a series of articles I have written. These include: Helen Marshall, 'Introduction,' in *The Year's Best Weird Fiction*, Vol. 4, eds. Helen Marshall and Michael Kelly (Toronto: Undertow Publications, 2017). Also see my discussion of King's work (drafted on this trip) at Helen Marshall, 'The Only Lights are Headlights,' *Weird Fiction Review*, August 10, 2016, http://weirdfictionreview.com/2016/08/101-weird-writers-43-stephen-king/.
2. Michael R. Collings and Stephen E. Fabian, *The Stephen King Phenomenon* (Mercer Island: Starmont House, 1987), 1.
3. This story has been recounted in a range of other articles and interviews, but I have found King's sense of the story here to be the fullest in *On Writing: A Memoir of the Craft* (New York: Scribner, 2000), 68.
4. Todorov's approach to the fantastic has informed my thinking on the nature of my writing although I frequently find myself butting up against the limitations of his definitions. See: Tzvetan Todorov, *The Fantastic: A Structural Approach to a Literary Genre*, trans. Richard Howard (Ithaca: Cornell University Press, 1973), 25.
5. Ibid., 31.
6. H.P. Lovecraft, 'The Call of Cthulhu,' in *The Call of Cthulhu and Other Weird Stories*, ed. S.T. Joshi (New York: Penguin Classics, 2002), 139.
7. Bruce Sterling, 'Catscan,' *SF Eye #5* (July 1989), accessed June 8, 2020, http://indbooks.in/mirror1/?p=311829. The nature of slipstream gets

good coverage in James P. Kelly and John Kessel, eds., *Feeling Very Strange: The Slipstream Anthology* (San Francisco: Tachyon Publications, 2006).
8. Ibid.
9. H.P. Lovecraft, *The Annotated Supernatural Horror in Literature*, ed. S.T. Joshi (New York: Hippocampus Press, 2000), 29.
10. A complete history of the emergence and analysis of weird fiction — with a particular emphasis on the new weird — is very beyond the remit of this essay. For reference, I have found the following works particularly useful. Ann VanderMeer, and Jeff VanderMeer, eds., *The Weird: A Compendium of Strange and Dark Stories* (New York: Tor Books, 2012); Jeffrey Andrew Weinstock, 'The New Weird,' in *New Directions in Popular Fiction: Genre, Reproduction, Distribution*, ed. Ken Gelder (Basingstoke: Palgrave Macmillan, 2016): 177–200; Joan Gordon, 'Reveling in Genre: An Interview with China Miéville,' *Science Fiction Studies* 30 (2003): 91; and Roger Luckhurst, 'The Weird: A Dis/orientation,' *Textual Practice* 31, no. 6 (2017): 1041–61.
11. Morton, *Hyperobjects*, 12.
12. *Ju-on: The Grudge*, directed by Takashi Shimizu (2003; Akasaka, Minato, Tokyo, Japan: Pioneer LDC), Blu-ray Disc, 1080p.
13. Morton, *Hyperobjects*, 43.
14. Marshall, 'Survival Strategies.' First published in *Black Static* 58 (TTA Press), 2017.
15. Morton, *Hyperobjects*, 87.
16. Charlie Stross, 'Why I Barely Read SF These Days,' *Charlie's Diary*, February 6, 2018, http://www.antipope.org/charlie/blog-static/2018/02/why-i-barely-read-sf-these-day.html.
17. Morton, *Hyperobjects*, 88.
18. Carl Maria Von Weber, 'On the Opera Undine,' *Allgemeine Musikalische Zeitung*, 19 (1817): 201–208, reprinted in *Source Readings in Music History: The Romantic Era*, trans. Oliver Strunk (London: Norton, 1965), 63.
19. This short essay — or collection of notes toward an essay — appears in its full form on *Reddit* though excerpts have been widely shared on the Internet in M. John Harrison (u/Biomancer), 'A Short Essay by the Great Sci-Fi Author M. John Harrison About Why Storytelling Must Take Precedence Over Worldbuilding,' *Reddit*, December 14, 2014.
20. Ibid.
21. Ibid.
22. Ibid.
23. *The Invitation*, directed by Karyn Kusama (2015; New York City, New York: Gamechanger Films), Blu-ray Disc, 1080p.

'A FLARE OF LIGHT OR THE GREAT CLOMPING FOOT OF NERDISM?'
M. JOHN HARRISON'S RADICAL POETICS OF WORLDBUILDING

First published in *TEXT: Journal of writing and writing courses* 24, 2 (October, 2020): 1-24.

'I remember [M. John Harrison] in conversation at the Institute for Contemporary Art trying to explain the nature of fantastic fiction to an audience: he described someone standing in a windy lane, looking at *the reflection of the world* in the window of a shop, and seeing, sudden and unexplained, a shower of sparks in the glass.'

(Gaiman 2005: xii, emphasis my own)

INTRODUCTION: THE REFLECTION OF THE WORLD

In January, 2007, M. John Harrison — old-school polemicist and 'one of the restless fathers of modern [science fiction]' (Macfarlane 2013) — kicked up an Internet storm when he proclaimed the worldbuilding of many of his contemporaries was 'the great clomping foot of nerdism' (2007b). Controverting the prevailing view in commercial science fiction and fantasy[1], he wrote:

> Every moment of a science fiction story must represent the triumph of writing over worldbuilding.

Worldbuilding is dull. Worldbuilding literalises the urge to invent. Worldbuilding gives an unneccessary [sic] permission for acts of writing (indeed, for acts of reading). Worldbuilding numbs the reader's ability to fulfil their part of the bargain, because it believes that it has to do everything around here if anything is going to get done (2007b).

Commenters on blogs, message boards and Reddit threads reacted with alacrity, some quizzical, others supportive; by and large, a torrent of invective followed. This included *ad hominem* attacks on 'a midlist author extremely jealous of the popularity and sales of the epic fantasy novelists' (St-Denis 2007) and criticisms of what was seen as a postmodernist or elitist rejection of traditional genre writing ('For better or worse, readers without literature degrees *tend to hate this stuff* [Bakker 2007]). As far as Internet discourse goes, so far, so predictable.

What puzzled some upon further reflection was the fact that Harrison *was* a skilled worldbuilder, immensely so. A casual rifling through the 2005 Bantam reprinting of some of his influential works confirms the status of Viriconium, sometimes known as The Pastel City, his fictional fantasy world. At a surface level little might distinguish Viriconium from the worlds of his contemporaries, as one reviewer pointed out when challenged to read Harrison's work in the wake of the continuing critical response to his post (Moher 2010). Like George R. R. Martin's Westeros or Steven Erikson's Malazan Empire, Viriconium differed from consensus reality in its history, its geography, and culture and Harrison had furnished it with richly-imagined details: the Artists' Quarter, the Gabelline Stairs, the Plaza of Unrealised Time, the Proton Circuit spiralling up to the sunset towers. But if Harrison appears to be a master worldbuilder himself, how then should we interpret his polemic against worldbuilding?

Over the last forty years, worldbuilding has become central to the art of writing science fiction and fantasy books. In his seminal study, Mark J. P. Wolf describes fictional worlds as 'dynamic entities' (2012: 3), which he regards as distinct from the narrative processes which create them. For Wolf, an imaginary world consists of

> the surroundings and places experienced by a fictional character (or which could be experienced by one) that together constitute a unified sense of place which is ontologically different from the actual, material, and so-called 'real' world. (2012: 377)

Although we can find examples of fictional worlds in early works such as Christine de Pizan's *The Book of the City of Ladies* (finished 1405) and Thomas More's *Utopia* (1516), it was early twentieth century fantasists such as George MacDonald, J. R. R. Tolkien and C. S. Lewis who first discussed the principles of '[inventing] a little world…with its own laws' (Macdonald 2004 [1890]: 65). In the decade following the success of the mass-market paperback of *The Lord of the Rings* trilogy in the 1965 and the subsequent growth of the fantasy genre, authors and editors discussed best practice for worldbuilding in guides such as Lin Carter's *Imaginary Worlds: The Art of Fantasy* (1973), Orson Scott Card's *How to Write Science Fiction and Fantasy* (1990) and Jeff VanderMeer's *Wonderbook* (2013).

Wolf's detailed study presents worldbuilding as an inherently pleasurable human activity and, increasingly, as a profoundly profitable feature of the media industry. Its centrality to media production has only grown with the franchisable potential of sprawling transmedia worlds such as those of *Star Wars* and *Star Trek*, which have each spawned complicated canons of work, across film, television, videogames and novels. In light of this, Henry Jenkins argues:

> More and more, storytelling has become the art of world-building, as artists create compelling environments that cannot be fully explored or exhausted within a single work or even a single medium. The world is bigger than the film, bigger than even the franchise—since fan speculations and elaborations also expand the world in a variety of directions. As an experienced screenwriter told me, 'When I first started, you would pitch a

story because within a good story, you didn't really have a film. Later, once sequels started to take off, you pitched a character because a good character could support multiple stories. And now, you pitch a world because a world can support multiple characters and multiple stories across multiple media.' (2006: 114)

Many writers have correspondingly laid out the skills they feel necessary to build a realistic, compelling and consumable world. A brief survey of online resources reveals an evolving body of advice regarding geography, geology, economics, linguistics and related subjects. (For a limited selection, see Holling 2001 and Anders 2003.) Good science fiction, these tend to argue, presents 'a fully realized, multidimensional vision, including not only the technological and scientific, but the psychological, cultural, moral, social, and environmental dimensions of future human existence' (Lombardo 2018: 3) and Wolf supports this by suggesting the goals to be pursued by worldbuilders are invention, completeness and internal consistency (2012: 33).

Ultimately, though, these sources offer little scepticism of worldbuilding, making Harrison's remarks particularly noteworthy. Yet in this scepticism Harrison taps into a rich vein of philosophical thought by scholars such as Guy Debord and Jean Baudrillard who critique media-produced 'hyperrealities', a term referring to 'the generation by models of a real without origin or reality', or the simulated realm that appears 'more real than the real' (Baudrillard 1994:1). Likewise, Harrison anticipates speculative realists such as Timothy Morton who, developing and complicating the ideas of Baudrillard, Heidegger and Husserl, rejects 'the world' in and of itself as an 'aesthetic effect based on a blurriness and aesthetic distance' (2013: 85), an effect that has evaporated in our modern era. Thus, when Morton suggests global warming will bring about 'the end of the world', he does not mean this in the traditional sense; rather he refers to the end of a certain way of thinking about 'the world' as 'a significant, bounded, horizoning entity' (2013: 87). According to Morton, we should be suspicious of artworks such as *The Lord of the Rings* with their seamless fictional worlds because they present false coherences. It is of interest then the extent to which Harrison and some of his contemporaries Michael Moorcock and China Miéville locate their own practice in relation to Tolkien, as I shall discuss.

Traces of this scepticism haunt contemporary science fiction writing. Take, for example, the popular science fiction writer Charlie Stross. In a recent blog post he quoted (and disagreed) with Harrison's polemic, reading it either as a wholesale rejection of any attempt to create plausible secondary worlds or else, as others have misinterpreted it, a privileging of story over setting. In favour of worldbuilding, he argued:

> The implicit construction of an artificial but plausible world is what distinguishes a work of science fiction from any other form of literature. It's an alternative type of underpinning to actually-existing reality, which is generally more substantial (and less plausible—reality is under no compulsion to make sense). Note the emphasis on *implicit*, though. Worldbuilding is like underwear: it needs to be there, but it shouldn't be on display, unless you're performing burlesque. Worldbuilding is the scaffolding that supports the costume to which our attention is directed. Without worldbuilding, the galactic emperor has no underpants to wear with his new suit, and runs the risk of leaving skidmarks on his story. (2018)

For Stross, worldbuilding is all-important to science fiction, the 'scaffolding' that makes it an effective form of storytelling. Yet Stross claims much recent science fiction prefers spectacle over plausibility, and in jettisoning plausibility, these stories lose their ability to critique the conditions of the world (ie. late stage capitalism) as we inhabit it. But in placing worldbuilding at the heart of 'good' science fiction, Stross creates a very different crisis for himself; for if, as he says, reality is under no compulsion to make sense, how can art *ever* produce a plausible and coherent yet realistic world? In fact, Stross wants the opposite of this sort of messy, inexplicable real-realism. Instead, he turns to fiction because 'world-building provides a set of behavioural constraints that make it *easier* to understand the character of my fictional protagonists' (2018). Therein lies the crux. In essence, Stross wants a world more plausible, more understandable, more realistic-than-the-real world — a hyperreality. When Stross rejects Harrison, he argues instead for worldbuilding as a tool for critique, but the underpinnings of that project are contradictory: extrapolating an explicable future from an inexplicable present. Yet Harrison, I will argue, is more sophisticated than Stross accepts: his approach recognises the fundamental 'unreality' of 'the real world' and indeed places this recognition at heart of his writing.

As market conditions prioritise fictional worlds that are extendible, franchisable, pleasurable and ultimately consumable, this paper argues for Harrison's importance in developing a poetics of scepticism toward worldbuilding. By poetics, I follow Robert Sheppard in seeing the reflective work of a writer as ongoing and elusive, strategic, born from crises, and often appearing in fragmentary forms: 'the snapshot, the epigraph, the embedded quotation, the scrawl on the back of on envelope' (2003) — to which one might easily add the Internet forum, the blog, the Reddit comments section. Simplistic readings of his polemic paint a picture of a writer dissatisfied with the prevailing market conditions, but this masks Harrison's deeper—and more provocative—dissatisfaction with the limitations of fiction. The trajectory of my discussion takes the form of a long, non-continuous arc with several creative, pedagogical interludes. The initial exploration focusses upon Harrison's early works and their relationship to epic fantasy and the New Wave, especially. This lays the groundwork for my discussion of the invention of the New Weird, a term Harrison coined not to name a thing that already existed, as many have argued, but rather to *create a space* for a thing he wanted: a radical subjectivity that would reframe the workings of science fiction and fantasy with particular respect to its worldbuilding. This attempt ultimately failed, as the New Weird, subject to the very processes of commodification and marketing Harrison urged his fellow writers to resist, rather perversely came to represent the opposite of what it had first pointed to. Threaded through my analysis is an attempt to come to terms with how his radical poetics is embedded in a complex struggle between craft, genre, market considerations as well as how it uses its own central contradictions as an engine, a mechanism to 'flare' the real world into existence (Harrison 1992[1989]: 149).

INTERLUDE I: AN EXERCISE IN WORLDBUILDING

In the Middle Ages, the itinerarium *was a common form of road map comprising a list of cities and their respective distances from one to the next. Often they recounted the journey to Jerusalem, appropriate for a pilgrimage.*

Imagine that you are about to embark on a voyage of your own. What are the names of the cities that you will pass on your journey from your own present location to the fabled city of Viriconium? Be sure to include intervening distances.

WHICH WAY TO VIRICONIUM? A PROBLEM OF NEW WORLDS AND THE NEW WAVE

Born in July 1945, M. John Harrison cut his teeth in the New Wave of speculative fiction. He published his first short story in 1966 in *Science Fantasy,* after which he relocated to London and met Michael Moorcock, the influential editor of *New Worlds* and an acclaimed fantasy writer. Two years later in 1968, Harrison became the books editor under Moorcock where he worked with authors like JG Ballard and Brian Aldiss to push science fiction and fantasy in experimental directions. This project had been ongoing for some time and Harrison admits by the time he arrived 'all the important work had been done' (2016). Four years earlier, in 1962, Ballard had published an editorial 'Which Way to Inner Space?' arguing that 'science fiction must jettison its present narrative forms and plots ... it is *inner* space, not outer, that needs to be explored' (2017[1962]: 117). Nevertheless, the work of the New Wave was a significant influence, particularly its mission to bust long-established genre tropes. An iconoclast at heart, Harrison took to this work with equal parts glee and vitriol. He used this time to 'identify the illusions central to the genre' (1992: 140). Language was his weapon of choice in puncturing these.

In 1971, he published *The Pastel City*, which took place in a Moorcockian high fantasy world. In a reflective essay he looks back upon this time as one in which he explored how fantasy-worlds with their focus on narratives of self-determination existed as places for action without consequences (1992[1989]: 140). During this stage of his career, he was still interested in the set-dressing of traditional high fantasy worlds, and he furnished *The Pastel City* with a prologue describing the history of the empire of Viriconium. It begins:

> Some seventeen notable empires rose in the Middle Period of Earth. These were the Afternoon Cultures. All but one are unimportant to this narrative, and there is little need to speak of them save to say that none of them lasted for less than a millennium, none for more than ten; that each extracted such secrets and obtained such comforts as its nature (and the nature of the universe) enabled it to find; and that each fell back from the universe in confusion, dwindled, and died. (Harrison 2005[1971]: 3)

It is of some note that writers frustrated by Harrison's scepticism of worldbuilding frequently find themselves startled by *The Pastel City*'s overt 'infodump' (Moher 2010), a technique often negatively associated with the encyclopaedic tendencies of worldbuilding to over-explain their settings. Yet Harrison's prologue is subtle, deliberately inhabiting the space of traditional fantasy only to subvert it. It suggests a scepticism of the amassed knowledge of Afternoon Cultures, which was bounded both by the nature of the universe and the nature of the epistemological constraints of the culture itself. Here we see an early glimpse of Harrison's project: worldbuilding which cannot divorce itself from an awareness of the limitations of 'the world'. Harrison further signals his interest in the gap between experienced 'world' and reality with his identification of his hero, tegeus-Cromis, as a man 'possessed by the essential quality of things than by their names; concerned with the reality of Reality, rather than with the names men gave it' (2005[1971]: 7). Thus, we see in Cromis a character seeking to look beyond 'the world'.

This scepticism of worlds appears in *The Pastel City* but finds a clearer articulation in Harrison's subsequent Viriconium novel *A Storm of Wings* (1980). Here we see the appearance of a cult known as the Sign of the Locust whose early converts maintained,

> The world is not as we perceive it...but infinitely more surprising. We must cultivate a diverse view.... We counterfeit the 'real,' ... by our very forward passage through time, and thus occlude the actual and essential. (2005[1980]: 126)

These interludes, brief as they are, appear like a voice from beyond the story itself, a crack in the conceptual framework, a leak: the storyworld acknowledging itself for a moment as storyworld. The Viriconium of this novel is not the same as *The Pastel City* though it seems chronologically linked; the geography changes, the nature of the world has shifted. *A Storm of Wings* reiterates the plot of *The Pastel City* in many respects: a group of heroes travel across the landscape in hopes of warding off the threat of invasion. In this case, the invasion comes in the form of enormous insects from the moon who have begun to build their own rival metropolis. They comprehend reality according to their own terms, and Harrison describes their alien *Umwelt* as 'immaculate and ravishing, a philosophy like a single drop of poison at the centre of a curved mirror...the first infection of the human reality' (2005[1980]: 225). Here he draws upon Jakob von Uexküll's notion of the *Umwelt*: a perspective of an environment 'built up through our sensory impressions and our actions in it' (Pak 2019: 195). There are limits to this cognitive reconstruction, one of which is the occlusion of rival worldviews

— precisely the threat posed by the invaders in *A Storm of Wings*. This book ushered in a phase of exploration in Harrison's writing in which he aimed to subvert the illusions of fantasy 'because to do so might be to reveal — for a fraction of a second, to yourself as much as the reader — the world the fictional illusion denies' (1992[1989]: 140). As readers we inhabit Viriconium, but Viriconium reminds us it is changeable, malleable, fragile, non-existent; it overlaps and erases; it is an unmappable world, a world which actively resists the project of the mapmaker.

Harrison's early works do not oppose generic fantasy tropes, but rather attempt to bend them back upon themselves. But in undertaking such a project, even with an ironic eye and a wilful frame of mind, he found himself dissatisfied with the sluggish tools of the genre: 'If you want to speak directly about — or to — what is human in people, it's no good learning sword-talk' (1992[1989]: 142). His subsequent years and final reviews for *New Worlds* grapple with this difficulty, as Latham discusses (2019 [2005]). 'Sweet Analytics', Harrison's 1975 capstone as books editor, excoriated fantasy works for creating substitute realities 'so lavish, so detailed and so long that they provide a complete 'world' for their audience' (Harrison 1975: 212). He saw these stories as providing 'some more or less easily-grasped handle by which to pick up the universe' (Harrison 1975: 212), a sentiment we see echoed in Stross's desire for fiction to make sense of a world that at times appears nonsensical. But Harrison preferred a mode of attack that would destabilise and unsettle, that would reveal the world as incoherent and painful. By the late 1970s, Harrison had turned away from both Moorcock and Ballard; by the mid-80s he had also rejected much of his own early work. One of the major problems of the New Wave, he later recognised, was that by rejecting the escapist elements many of science fiction and fantasy readers wanted, its authors were in fact destroying their own commercial appeal: 'sawing through the bough' they were sitting on, so to speak (Darlington 1983). And as he began to reject the project of the New Wave, he himself faced the same challenge. The result was a new understanding of his own goals and a new paradox. He saw fantasy as a genre in which

> ...we can never escape the world. We cannot stop trying to escape the world.... We learn to run away from fantasy and into the world, write fantasies at the heart of which by some twist lies the very thing we fantasise against. (1992 [1989]: 140-141)

For ten years he would explore rejections of fantasy, publishing a 'realist' novel called *Climbers* in 1989. He appeared to turn away from the fantastic and its attempts to interpose a metaphor between reader and subject; yet this was not the case, exactly. Realism too — any form of fiction — seemed fraught by the same issues of representation, the creation of hyperrealities. By the end of the 80s he found within this self-contradiction 'an engine, like all scandals, a source of power' (1992 [1989]: 147). The tendency toward escape was not a problem that could be solved but an energy that could be used. Indeed, his work can best be seen as an attempt to grapple with this central contradiction without abandoning the project of writing as a whole.

INTERLUDE II: AN EXERCISE IN WORLDBUILDING

Imagine, to escape a storm, you have just bundled your way into the Café Californium, an outpost and common waypoint in the Artists' Quarter of Uriconium. Instantly you are approached by an old man who offers you good food to keep you happy while the storm passes. What food does he offer you? Of what is it composed? Bring vividly to mind its heat, the balance of its spices, the texture of its components.

Now imagine yourself outside in the street, having never entered (or have you? maybe once, not recently). Briefly, you watch what passes through a window as the rain slicks the glass. Inside the cafe, you see a traveller bought some exotic, steaming dish. From your vantage point in the street, you cannot help but imagine yourself as the traveller. What does the first bite of food taste like?

THE NEW WEIRD: FENCES, REFLECTIONS, ENCLOSURES

The early aughts witnessed a revolution of sorts; a revolution not in terms of the overthrowing of the old, but rather a revolution in the technical, linguistic sense: a turning back, a full rotation. The 1990s had seen a 'boom' in British science fiction writing (Butler, 2003). At the forefront of these was China Miéville whose Bas Lag series (*Perdido Street Station,* 2000; *The Scar,* 2002; *Iron Council,* 2004) brought him a rare mixture of commercial and critical acclaim. The success of *Perdido Street Station* in particular 'both coarsened and broadened' (VanderMeer 2008: xi) a set of techniques that had been common to earlier writers including Mervyn Peake and Harrison himself which included the disruption of traditional worldbuilding in favour of more experimental approaches. The New Wave had dissipated but the New Weird was building, not a literary school or organised movement, but rather a series of tendencies and impulses in a range of writings that echoed and advanced those of the New Wave.

It was just over thirty years since Harrison had begun to trouble the project of epic fantasy with *The Pastel City*; yet epic fantasy had persisted, commercially dominant, in the works of Robert Jordan, Steven Erikson, George R. R. Martin and others. If anything, it had been bolstered in the early aughts by the cinematic adaptations of *The Lord of the Rings*, which monumentally and spectacularly literalised Tolkien's storyworld. These adaptations were invested not only in the creation (or recreation of Middle Earth), but with a complex marketing machinery which Mathijs describes:

> Underpinning the experience of seeing the films ... was a promotional campaign of behemoth proportions — beginning prior to the opening of *The Fellowship of the Ring* and running through to the extended version of *The Return of the King* —

carried through with unflagging commercial zeal. The films were further endorsed by an almost four-year-long marketing bonanza which resulted in a tidal wave of books, magazines and comics, limited-edition artworks, two-a-penny toys, fast-food tie-ins and a seemingly limitless supply of gewgaws, gimcracks and miscellaneous knick-knackery. (2006: xvii)

No longer was *The Lord of the Rings* a textual phenomenon; it had become a high-value transmedia world proliferated in a range of media whose props, costumes and sets — the literal furniture of the movies — were available to be mimicked, replicated, and visited in a touring exhibition from 2003-2007. But there were signs that readers were willing to try something fresh. Miéville had broken through and his world — New Crobuzon, an admixed, hybrid city on the edge of scrub and marshland, part Victorian London, part Cairo and New Orleans — looked nothing like Middle Earth.

In 2003, Harrison posted on the now defunct message board of TTA Press with the words: 'The New Weird. Who does it? What is it? Is it even anything?' (VanderMeer 2008: 317). It was a provocative question. Harrison himself had first used the term to introduce Miéville's novella, *The Tain* (2002); now it seemed was a time to expand upon the space for change Miéville had opened up, to find allies. With this call to arms, he launched a heady discussion that rumbled on for close to three months and saw a number of writers attempt to define, clarify, and resist the term. To this date the message board discussions themselves provide a clearest sense of the tenuousness of the moment, its contradictions, a flowing conversation rather than a channelled discussion aimed at setting an agenda (a purpose Harrison rejected on multiple occasions). The writer Steph Swainston was one of the earliest commentators and her response offers the best description of the phenomenon to which Harrison was pointing:

The New Weird is a kickback against jaded heroic fantasy which has been the only staple for far too long. Instead of stemming from Tolkien, it is influenced by *Gormenghast* and *Viriconium*.

It is incredibly eclectic, and takes ideas from any source. It borrows from American Indian and Far Eastern mythology rather than European or Norse traditions, but the main influence is modern culture—street culture—mixing with ancient mythologies. The text isn't experimental, but the creatures are. It is amazingly empathic.... (VanderMeer 2008: 319)

The New Weird's rejection of Tolkien had its roots in Moorcock's 1978 essay 'Epic Pooh'. There, the architect of the New Wave had criticised Tolkien's claim that *The Lord of the Rings* was 'primarily linguistic in its conceptions, that there were no symbols or allegories' (1978: 6). Moorcock saw in Tolkien a project of worldbuilding which sought to hide its master's Toryish worldview through a notional appearance of realism (linguistic and cultural coherence). Like Swainston, Miéville was deeply suspicious of the 'contagious' nature of Tolkien's tropes and his insistence on consolation as the goal of fantasy:

That is a revolting idea, and one, thankfully, that plenty of fantasists have ignored. From the Surrealists through the pulps — via Mervyn Peake and Mikhael Bulgakov and Stefan Grabinski and Bruno Schulz and Michael Moorcock and M. John Harrison and I could go on — the best writers have used the fantastic aesthetic precisely to challenge, to alienate, to subvert and undermine expectations. (2002b)

Yet despite his rejection of Tolkien's world, in *The Socialist Review*, Miéville praised Tolkien for introducing 'an extraordinary element of rigour to the genre' (2002a). For Miéville what was at stake was the very nature of fantasy as a tool for social critique. Only with rigorous worldbuilding, he argued, could fantasy allows its readers to understand the "absurdity' of capitalist modernity' (2004 [2002]: 337-339). To do so, fantasy needed to create internally coherent structures that its readers would recognise as impossible; this would equip those same readers to confront the self-perpetuating fantasy of capitalism. In this approach, we find an echo of Stross's anxiety that reality is under no compunction to make sense, yet where Stross would create an apparently plausible future world to make sense of its inconsistencies, Miéville found in the tension between not-real but believable and real but not-believable a useful way of enlivening readers to the gaps and fissures of the capitalist 'world'. If Miéville's approach to the New Weird might be summed up then, it would not a rejection of Tolkien's worldbuilding — 'his literalised fantastic of setting' (2005) — but rather a rejection of the moralist, abstract logic which structured the building of that world. For Miéville, this was all so much 'aesthetic and thematic furniture' (2005) and his interest with the New Weird was not so much in tearing down the walls as redecorating.

If Miéville looms large in this stage of the discussion, this is because it is his work more than Harrison's that drove the aesthetic of the New Weird. Swainston identified the dominant trait of New Weird books as their details: 'jewel-bright, hallucinatory, carefully described' (VanderMeer 2008: 317):

> These details — clothing, behaviour, scales and teeth — are what makes New Weird worlds so much like ours, as recognisable and as well-described. It is visual, and every scene is packed with baroque detail. Nouveau-goths use neon and tinsel as well as black clothes. The New Weird is more multi-spectral than gothic. (Ibid.)

Her description of these 'jewel-bright' details cannot help but evoke a sense of hoarding, fetishisation, enchantment, those same elements which made Tolkien's world so ripe for commodification. Rather than the glitter of chainmail, the New Weird preferred the glitter of a mantis or spider, some other mesmerising but horrific creature. Likewise, those who aligned themselves with the New Weird preferred the Gothic to Romance, enjoying both their structural principles (organic, decay, confusion) and their aesthetic (the hybrid, the grungy, the decadent). They found their roots in the shifting, phantasmagorical landscapes of Gormenghast and Viriconium rather than the tidier, romanticised hills of the Cotswolds.

Despite Harrison's scepticism of secondary worlds, attempts to come to some sort of description of the New Weird — a canon, a list of features that would make it recognisable, a coherent body of thought — focused very much on the furniture (the baroque, 'jewel-bright' details) of their worlds, with the understanding that the furniture is the most easily replicable stuff, the stuff that makes a new subgenre recognisable. Swainston seems to acknowledge this point when she asked, 'Do we have to wait for parodies of Bas-Lag?' (VanderMeer 2008: 319) and the anthologist Jonathan Strahan echoed it: 'If I have an unconscious motive [in resisting the label], it's not to ... live through a decade of people with very little talent dressing their latest trilogy up in new weird drag' (VanderMeer 2008: 328). There was a tension — sometimes enjoyable, sometimes disruptive — between the furniture of genre fiction (its recognisable elements) and what it might accomplish as a radical new mode. Like Harrison, Miéville wanted to use the tropes of genres he had enjoyed as a child to do more profound work. In his case, the pulps were a source of inspiration ('monsters and gunfights' [2005]). But in trying to mash pulpy and experimental styles together, even Miéville was willing to admit that the opposing values of these two systems had the potential to erode one another:

> Even if it's true that the different values fundamentally work against each other, the attempt to marry them may never succeed, but it might approach success asymptotically. Try again, fail again, fail better. That tension, that process of failing better and better — the very failure, if it's the best kind of failure — might generate interesting effects that a more 'successful' — i.e. aesthetically integrated — work cannot do. (2005)

Harrison, of course, had made a similar journey, trying to use the tropes of fantasy for his own ends. But in the eighties, he had come to feel the techniques of popular fiction had an 'inertia' (142). So it seems difficult for me to believe that what he was searching for in the New Weird was another set of furniture. In fact, it was the opposite. Thus we should read Harrison's foray, not as a way of constructing a commercial zone for himself, but rather as a way of deliberately de-commercialising his work and that of his contemporaries, while at the same time claiming it:

> ...in misreading my opening post ... you underestimate not just the cheerful ironic glee of new-movement-name; you underestimate the amount of agenda involved. If I don't throw my hat in the ring, write preface, do a guest editorial here, write a review in the *Guardian* there, then I'm leaving it to Michael Moorcock or David Harwell to describe what I (and the British authors I admire) write.... The struggle to name is the struggle to own. (VanderMeer 2008: 323)

He wanted to claim responsibilities for his ideas, set the stage for an imagined battle over naming to come, and most importantly, to identify a new form of fiction that would be suited for addressing the next decade's turn toward fantasy (and perhaps science fiction) as the substance of life. If in the past the tools of fantasy had felt too sluggish and inert to address human issues, perhaps with the turn of the century and the growth of fantastic new hyperrealities, this was the moment when they would be necessary.

INTERLUDE III: AN EXERCISE IN WORLDBUILDING

Write a brief account of the founding of Vriko.
   Write a new version of this for every year of the next decade.
   Prepare a short essay examining alternations in chronology and noticeable divergence points.

. . .

Marks will be awarded on the basis of originality, seriousness of purpose, and rigour.

WHAT'S IN A NAME? THE OLD WEIRD, NEW WEIRD AND AFTERWEIRD

Thus, Harrison's battle for names began; largely, it was lost.

In 2008, Ann and Jeff VanderMeer edited *The New Weird* anthology which provided a list of names including Miéville, Swainston, Moorcock and Harrison and reprinted an excerpt from the discussion of the TTA message boards. In this anthology, what Harrison had identified as a primarily British phenomenon was widened; connections were made with European writers such as Felix Gilman and Leena Krohn as well as Americans like Michael Cisco and Jeff VanderMeer himself who had contributed to the message board. In a series of short essays by European editors, the New Weird movement, which started as provocation, devolved into a flabby marketing category comprising some form of cross-genre experimentation, often with literary techniques (Šust et al 2008, 351, 352). Perhaps because of the American influence, the science fiction angle (authors such as Alastair Reynolds) was replaced with a more overt focus on horror, connecting with a separate regrowth of the Lovecraftian Weird exemplified by American writers such as Laird Barron and John Langan. Three years later in 2011, the (again) American short story writer Scott Nicolay posted his 'Dogme 2011 for Weird Fiction' which demonstrated the substantial shift which had occurred. He banned anthropomorphic monsters, stock figures from noir, post-apocalyptic scenarios, buzzwords from H. P. Lovecraft, the trappings of steampunk amongst other furniture apparently considered part of the subgenre. In its place, he suggested the importance of place ('Scout and employ real locations whenever possible'), atmosphere, and low-lighting ('the tale must suggest more than it describes'). If Swainston had argued for the New Weird's 'vivacity, vitality, detail' (VanderMeer 2008: 319), then by

2011 the mantra had become unease, exanimation, and obfuscation.

Clearly something was going on. That same year, Peter Straub edited *Poe's Children: The New Horror,* which named Harrison as a progenitor in combining elements of traditional horror with

> the use of deliberate narrative devices, including unreliable narrators, stories-within-stories, metatextual layering of narratives, shifting points of view, self-conscious allusiveness, and often surprising dissonances of tone and style (Wolfe 2011: 152).

This simultaneous 'evaporation' of genres, to use Wolfe's phrase, took place alongside a notable attempt to reconfigure and remarket the liminal space opened up in association with weird fiction. The next year saw the publication of the landmark anthology *The Weird Compendium* (2012), edited by Jeff and Ann VanderMeer. They expanded the definition of the Weird and traced the movement back to the Lovecraft Circle of Robert E. Howard, Fritz Leiber, Clark Ashton Smith, Howard Wandrei, and August Derleth. This marked the importance of a rather different set of furniture. In 2008, Miéville had described the tentacle as 'the default monstrous appendage of today, [signalling] the epochal shift to a Weird culture' (2011); and he was right in not only his critique of modernity but his presentiment of the importance of the imagery. By 2012 the VanderMeers highlighted the tentacle's omnipresence in modern weird writing. They admitted the influence of Surrealism, Symbolism, Decadent Literature, the New Wave, and the more esoteric strains of the Gothic; found echoes of it in the New Waves works of Moorcock, Ballard and Harrison; and argued for its re-emergence via Miéville who synthesised 'the tentacle horrors of Lovecraft with the intellectual rigor of the New Wave' (2012: xx). In 2014, Nicolay pushed for a further re-alignment by relabelling the convergent strands the 'Weird Renaissance' which he intended to be a label broad enough to capture all of this innovation. By that point the discussions which had been prompted by a set of British writers experimenting with amalgamations of science fiction and fantasy had morphed into a largely American-centric resuscitation of Lovecraft, furnished with a suite of anthologies, which would be published over the next several years. These included *Lovecraft Unbound*, ed. Ellen Datlow (2015); *The Mammoth Book of Original Cthulhu*, ed. Paula Guran (2016) and *Children of Lovecraft*, ed. Ellen Datlow (2016). By the end of 2016 the movement had become a marketing label and Strahan's fears of a generation of 'new weird drag' (now Cthulhu rather than Gormenghast) had been firmly realised.

But the failure of the New Weird as movement, moment and marketing category —or perhaps its rehabilitation as the last in a changed but evidently viable form — hides what the discussion did accomplish. In my mind, the critic Jonathan McCalmont identifies this best in his sophisticated exploration of the TTA message board threads:

> What these discussions contain is something far more primal and basic than the emergence of a genre; what they reflect is the troubled birth of a new literary subjectivity.... One so raw and unformed that it was not ready to yield the sort of practical outcomes demanded by the wider genre community or the commercial interests attached to it. (2016)

This is vital to our discussion: what Harrison did — or tried to do — with his discussion was open up a space for a new form of writing, not by creating a trendy marketing label but by forging links between otherwise unlike writers who believed the tools for making meaning could be refashioned. McCalmont argues that

> a shared response to a shared cultural moment can yield new techniques, new forms, new arguments, and new styles of collective action but before any of these productive outcomes

can take place, people need to realise that they are not alone. (2016)

Ultimately, Harrison tried to provoke a rethinking of genre and its necessity. But what did this radical new subjectivity look like? Nearing the end of the TTA message board discussion, author Justina Robson notes:

> I think that we've realised that there are 2 things going on in this discussion — one is the writing of realism-bending fiction and one is the philosophical enquiry about the nature of inner reality and its projection into the outside world. For the writing side, I think we've said all we can say. On the philosophical side I think there's a long way to go. (2003)

It is this philosophical strand that seems most clearly embedded in Harrison's rejection of worldbuilding as 'the clomping foot of nerdism', a perspective anticipated in the early New Weird discussions.

Thus, we circle around from the market conditions and back to the philosophical inquiry — and indeed back to Harrison's 2007 polemic against worldbuilding. In his subsequent blog posts, which expand and clarify his position, Harrison draws upon Baudrillard to argue that much contemporary worldbuilding with its focus on rationality and order

> ...undercuts the best and most exciting aspects of fantastic fiction, subordinating the uncontrolled, the intuitive & the authentically imaginative to the explicable; and replacing psychological, poetic & emotional logic with the rationality of the fake. (2007c)

With their need to project apparent realism, he believed writers such as Tolkien resisted the idea of writing as a game played between writers and readers: they installed a 'secondary creation' and ignored 'the genuine sleight-of-hand pleasures of conjuring in favour of a belief in magic, a kind of non-writing which claims to be rather than to simulate' (2007c). Harrison, on the other hand, lived for the game. So far so good, but what does this game look like it? We might see an echo of it in *The Pastel City* whereby the hero tegeus-Cromis, interested in the Reality of things, still demands from a strange visitor his name before they are able to converse (2005: 11). We might find another echo in Harrison's provocative labelling of the New Weird as well as his resistance to those trying to attach a clear referent to the label, resulting in the rejection of one set of agendas after another. This strategy seems to admit that although names are not good substitutions for Reality, nevertheless, they allow us to interact.

Where does that leave us in terms of a consideration of practice then? I will briefly sum up three alternatives discussed so far. The first is that of Miéville. As we have seen, Miéville did not reject worldbuilding; in fact, if anything he believed the radical potential of speculative fiction lay within its power to construct worlds. Miéville saw in *The Lord of the Rings* Tolkien's attempt to turn his back on 'the truth of post-traumatic Modernity' (2005): its collapse as a rational, humane system. In the works of Lovecraft, who Miéville positions as a foil, he saw an awareness of the same collapse:

> These different approaches manifest in their fantasies. To put it with unfair crudeness, Tolkien's is the fantasy of a man murmuring to himself 'it's alright, it's alright', but not believing it; Lovecraft's of a man shrieking 'none of it is alright, nor will it ever be'. (2005)

For him, then, a fantastic world does not offer escape from capitalism modernity. Fantasy mirrors it, but in so doing it interrogates the relationship between belief and reality. It allows its readers to see worlds as constructed and mediated; the better the world, the more plausibly constructed, the greater the potential for recognition of the complexity and artificiality of capitalist modernity.

The second approach is that of Jeff VanderMeer. In his writing guide *Wonderbook* he offers what is perhaps the most thoughtful integration of scepticism toward traditional worldbuilding. In addition to the commonplace advice about coherency, consistency, logic and detail, he argues for sufficient mystery and unexplored vistas, consistent inconsistency, multicultural representation, extended, literalised metaphors, multiple operational realities, collective and individual memory, and imperfect comprehension. 'The world' of the story in that sense must be polysemous: 'The places and spaces in which story occurs are not inert or merely backdrops to action — they have energy, motion, and create certain effects depending on your approach' (2013: 241). Such a practice offers avenues for incorporating a politicised understanding of the way in which a setting might be constructed from multiple overlapping and conflicting worldviews.

The third comes from Timothy Morton whom I have discussed briefly. Morton's work in speculative realism is informed by horror, hauntology and the weird; he argues that as we approach a period of environmental collapse, the end of 'the world' is inevitable. In this sense, 'the world' — which might be read as capitalist modernity, although it surely could not be limited to that — vanishes, and we are left with intimacy:

> Because when you look at the stars and imagine life on other planets, you are looking through the spherical glass screen of the atmosphere at objects that appear to be behind that glass screen — for all the developments since Ptolemy, in other worlds, you still imagine that we exist on the inside of some pristine glass sphere. The experience of cosmic wonder is an aesthetic experience, a three-dimensional surround version of looking at a picturesque painting in an art gallery. (2013: 108-109)

Intimacy for Morton is the sense that global warming and other such hyperobjects are not behind the glass screen; rather it's 'as if the glass screen starts to extrude itself toward you in a highly uncanny, scary way that violates the normal aesthetic propriety' (2013: 109). As our perception of 'the world' as a mediating element falls away, so too does the self. This intimacy involves 'not a sense of belonging to something bigger' but 'a sense of being close, even too close, to other lifeforms, of having them under one's skin' (2013: 113). Intimacy means apprehension without the safety of a 'world' to create a sense of distance.

How does Harrison's position knock up against these? Like Miéville and Morton, Harrison believes 'the world' has already been built up as a hyperreal environment by corporate ads and branding exercises, and thus worldbuilding is an inherently political argument, 'made even more urgent as a heavily-mediatised world moves from the prosthetic to the virtual, allowing the massively managed and flattered contemporary self to ignore the steady destruction of the actual world on which it depends' (2007c). Harrison's rejection of worldbuilding is not a rejection of the corporatisation of fictional worlds, then; it is a deeper rejection of readers believing — and enjoying — built worlds as if they were real. Thus, in his oeuvre, Viriconium persisted as a point of return in his writings, a site of further testing and twisting, a space that could be continually overwritten, that *had* to be continually overwritten, suffused with decay, degilded and coarsened. The degradation of Viriconium from *The Pastel City* to *A Storm of Wings* and onward was an aesthetic move in itself, an attempt to make the world unlivable, uninhabitable. This was in large part because Harrison recognised the city's charisma, which Fraser astutely argues, 'must be understood, paradoxically, as a caution against seductive charisma. To navigate this inscape demands not that we resolve its contradictions, but that we embrace them and enter into the spaces between them' (2019: 62). Harrison's penultimate short story 'A Young Man's Journey to Viriconium' describes this charismatic pull. It is suffused with a sense of loss, of the aborted escape. It echoes Rilke's description of a man for whom 'in a moment more, everything will have lost its meaning, and that table and the cup, and the chair to which he clings, all the near and commonplace things around him, will have become intelligible, strange and burdensome' (2005: 543). This is the vital experience of Viriconium: this undoing of intelligence, the loss of meaning of the objects which would give a life substance. This is a world in which the furniture is losing its ability to generate meaning at all. Harrison's writing no longer provides a route of escape from the real to the fantastical, but a rope leading the reader of the fantastic back toward the real.

But it is a difficult position for a fantasy writer to take. It seems to provoke the reader who comes to the text in search of relief from anxiety; it asks the reader who flees the complexities of the real world to encounter them again. But in doing so, what Harrison argues for is the power of literature to revitalise through a different kind of encounter with intimacy than that of Morton. He says:

> We begin by trying out illusions. Once we accept that illusions 'blind but do not hold', that we have at our disposal finally only the worldness of the world, then we find some way of 'escaping' into that. We learn to love what we longed to run from. We learn to run away from fantasy and into the world, write fantasies at the heart of which by some twist lies the very thing we fantasise-against.
>
> This hurts. (1992 [1989]: 141)

If fiction offers an escape, it is not an escape from pain; it is rather the awareness that this pain is the experience of life and that it is the purpose of fiction to reflect its painful contradictions, not to resolve them, but to flare them in our minds.

INTERLUDE IV: AN EXERCISE IN WORLDBUILDING

Choose seven objects in the same room as you now — yes, any seven objects. Do not be too careful in your consideration of them. There, these are yours to build with. Make a ladder. Make a mirror. Make an argument.

Make Viriconium.

1. The terminology for science fiction and fantasy is deeply contested, with diverging and occasionally converging approaches dependent on formal characteristics, market conditions, and other qualities. As the bending of genres and importance of market labels plays a major role in this essay, rather than preferring an umbrella term such as 'speculative fiction' (itself contested), I have instead tried to follow the self-identification and usage of the authors themselves. Consequently, it should be noted there are discrepancies and inconsistencies; while I have not made an effort to resolve these (and indeed feel such a resolution would only undermine Harrison's approach to constructive ambiguity), I have made an effort to provide clarity for the reader at points in which the traditions and practices seem to diverge most noticeably.

ON LAST YEAR'S LANGUAGE

First published in Years Best Weird Fiction, volume 4, 2017

For last year's words belong to last year's language
And next year's words await another voice.
And to make an end is to make a beginning.

—T.S. ELIOT, 'LITTLE GIDDING'

I come to this Introduction from a somewhat strange perspective. I was one of the people who woke up on November 9, 2016 — as a Canadian living in England, whose eyes were still fixed south of the border, across the pond — in what seemed to be an alternate reality.

The morning of the general election, I remember logging on and experiencing almost a doubling of vision, as if the universe had split into two tracks that were radically diverging from one another. There was a hallucinatory space of about a week where I still felt as if I could see another world layered underneath mine. There was shock and disorientation, not a little fear — but also bewilderment at how fragile the norms and traditions which formed the bedrocks of reality — *my* reality, as it turned out — had proven to be.

I don't mean to rehash politics. The tumultuous events of the last twelve months have been a shock to the system as one by one our certainties about the way things are have been cast aside. New futures have been dreamed up and rapidly discarded. Tiny bubbles of consensual realities have surfaced and burst, or gained power, grown, come to englobe more and more people. The speed of change has been rapid, disorienting. But in the wake of all this I've begun to think about my own experiences critically as a way of examining what literature is and what it ought to do.

I grew up in a little town in Ontario, on the border with Port Huron, Michigan, and so I'm used to border crossings. I have two passports, and this means I can pass easily, more easily than most, choosing whichever identity is most likely to be granted access. I know that liminal spaces are dangerous, and multiple identities can be useful — but they are also cause for suspicion. If you are two things — or three things, or many things — then you are not easily *one* thing; you can pass but you still present a risk. And increasingly, as I've crossed borders over the last year, I've registered a radical sense of difference, as the cultures of three countries I've felt as familiar as breathing have shifted and re-aligned.

Weird fiction is a strange beast, an eclectic genre (or subgenre). It originated in the late nineteenth and early twentieth century through the works of authors including Edgar Allan Poe, Arthur Machen, and M. R. James, amongst others, and has since developed over the course of the last hundred years to encompass new writers such as China Miéville, M. John Harrison and others. Weird fiction is notable for its generic uncertainty; it exists at the boundary between science fiction and horror — perhaps — or between literary fiction and horror — perhaps — or between Lovecraft and whatever happens to be floating close to hand at any given moment — perhaps!

In 1933, in the lull between two world wars, a year which included the death of President Calvin Coolidge, an assassination attempt on President-elect Franklin D. Roosevelt, the beginning of the Great Depression and the premiere of the original film version of *King Kong* at Radio City Music Hall, a middle-aged pulp writer by the name of H. P. Lovecraft began work on an article addressing weird fiction which would later be published in the June 1937 issue of the *Amateur Correspondent*. 'I choose weird stories', he wrote, 'because they suit my inclination best — one of my strongest and most persistent wishes being to achieve, momentarily, the illusion of some strange suspension or violation of the galling limitations of time, space, and natural law which forever imprison us and frustrate our curiosity about the infinite cosmic spaces beyond the radius of our sight and analysis.' In this article Lovecraft sketched out the parameters of a kind of story interested in using the language of dreams and fragments, vague impressions, snatches of scientific discourse, in order to interrogate the nature of reality. This work, whatever we may think of the man himself and his influence on the field now, both of which have deservedly (in my opinion) required re-evaluation, is still ongoing — and still necessary.

In fact, it would seem that in our moment this work is more necessary than ever.

Recently, another short story writer interested in the nature of reality had something to say about the nature of catastrophic change. In 2011, Dominican author Junot Díaz interrogated the response to the devastating earthquake in Haiti in an article entitled 'Apocalypses: What Disasters Reveal' in *The Boston Review*. He wrote of the etymology of the word 'apocalypse', which means 'to uncover and unveil.' There are three kinds of apocalypses, he argues: there are those that follow the actual imagined end of the world; there are those that comprise catastrophes which *resemble* the imagined end; and there are those disruptive events that provoke revelation. The apocalypse, he says, quoting James Berger, 'is the End, or resembles the end, or explains the end.'

We are, by all accounts, no matter where you might fit yourself in the political spectrum, in an apocalyptic moment. We are witnessing the end of something, or an event that resembles it; we are searching for an account that can explain that end.

On the day following the announcement of the results of the American election I was teaching a group of writers at Anglia Ruskin University. It was an evening class. The students had always been a lively bunch, eager, full of questions and comments and jokes and affection for one another. But that day I didn't know how to address them. One colleague had told me not to talk about Trump, to just leave it out of the room, but that seemed impossible. Politics, whatever we believe, is at the heart of writing; it is a vital part of living and participating in society.

I did the best thing I could think of in the situation. I cribbed something I'd heard from Ben Markovits, a lecturer at Royal Holloway: that the purpose of teaching creative writing is, on the one hand, to help students to become published (in the best cases) — but in all cases, regardless of the quality of the writing, it is *to help students to become better witnesses to the world*. I have thought hard on that maxim since I first heard it. We are all witnesses of the world. The tools of storytelling can help us, in this respect: they help us to understand our world, to observe it, to *process* it. This is a fundamentally imaginative act and it is an act with great power — the power to witness.

We are living in an apocalyptic moment and we have a duty to be witnesses. We have a duty to observe, to imagine, to speculate, and to create.

Weird fiction is a genre that knows about the apocalypse.

It is a genre used to dismantling the status quo and exploring what lies beyond the margins of what is known in the world. It is genre obsessed with bringing to light what wishes to remain hidden and dealing with the consequences of that revelation.

The rules of reality have changed. This is an age in which it seems impossible to count on shared assumptions. Gary Dunion on Twitter cleverly captured the zeitgeist by pulling together a number of headlines he had read recently:

- Suspect in North Korea killing 'thought she was taking part in TV prank'
- Robert Mugabe could contest election as corpse, wife says
- German parents told to destroy doll that can spy on children

His caption? *Season 4 of Black Mirror is coming along nicely...* Indeed.

The Twitter account for *Black Mirror* states: 'Our job is to explain what's happening to you as best we can.' As we have seen, it's becoming increasingly difficult to distinguish between fact and fiction. I can only imagine the problem is going to get worse.

When Lovecraft talked about his short stories he imagined fear to be at the heart of the process of discovery and revelation. He said:

> These stories frequently emphasise the element of horror because fear is our deepest and strongest emotion, and the one which best lends itself to the creation of nature-defying illusions. Horror and the unknown or the strange are always closely connected, so that it is hard to create a convincing picture of shattered natural law or cosmic alienage or 'outsideness' without laying stress on the emotion of fear. The reason why *time* plays a great part in so many of my tales is that this element looms up in my mind as the most profoundly dramatic and grimly terrible thing in the universe. *Conflict with time* seems to me the most potent and fruitful theme in all human expression.

In this respect, weird fiction seems a perfect vehicle for exploring our present moment. For it does seem to us, I think, to many of us, anyway, that time is out of joint; are we moving back to the happy utopia of the 1950s? Are we moving toward the dystopia of *1984*? Are we returning or progressing? We do not know. We cannot decide. And the possibilities are not so much divergent as layered overtop of one another. We are existing in multiple moments at once, in multiple *times* at once.

And it is *scary*.

Ann and Jeff VanderMeer, in their introduction to *The Weird* compendium, recognise the murky taxonomy of weird fiction writing:

> Because The Weird often exists in the interstices, because it can occupy different territories simultaneously, an impulse exists among the more rigid taxonomists to find The Weird suspect, to argue it should not, cannot be, separated out from other traditions.

Weird fiction then is used to this strange overlapping, this occupation of simultaneous moments at once. It is a revelatory mode of writing, an apocalyptic mode of writing.

This volume was edited with the assistance of a group of students from my university who read through the solicited stories, made recommendations, debated the value of individual pieces and applied — and often questioned — the definition of weird fiction to them. Though the final selections were my own, our conversations shaped my thinking. One particular definition resonated strongly with me. It came from Marian Womack, a specular Spanish short story writer and translator whose work has appeared in a previous volume of this series.

She said:

> We have a long tradition of [The Weird] in Spain, and this only increased during the dictatorship as new symbolic ways of communicating ideas were rehearsed in narratives (cinematic and literary). This kind of fantasy, in which 'something is not quite right', lends itself very well to Gothic sensibility, with its convoluted use of language and its tormented heroes. And then there is an element of irrationality built into the rational and, coming from a Spanish background, I interpret this as

surrealism, for me this is a major element I recognise in weird writing, and one that is present in my own understanding of the weird.

Her response pointed away from, not toward, Lovecraft; it sketched out other directions for inquiry, other crises, other narratives, other points of view than those in which weird fiction has been traditionally grounded. Yet her definition struck me as capturing the essence of the weird tale, the embedding of irrationality within the rational: a way of writing which uses the one to expose the other, to make the reader realise that all supposedly rational systems are inherently irrational.

In thinking about the state of the genre, I'm reminded of an article written by a provocative critic, Jonathan McCalmont, who traced the history of the resurgence of weird fiction in the twentieth century. In particular, he focused on several months in 2003 in Britain when the TTA Press message boards were alive with a great discussion about the nature of the 'New Weird'. The discussion was prompted in part by the success of Miéville who published *The Scar* in 2002 and received critical acclaim in the British Fantasy Award and Locus Awards of 2013.

The topic under debate was the rise of a new type of writing that seemed to have links with the past — a writing to which critics had begun to apply the label 'New Weird' — but the forum conversations were riven with arguments from critics and authors alike. M. John Harrison succinctly summed up the problem. A lively figure who emerged as part of the New Wave in the 60s and 70s, he had seen the dangers of labelling a movement. He felt as if the energy of the writing might well be diminished through successive waves of commercialization:

> ...once the New Wave parameters were codified, there was a general softening-off as second generation writers stripped out the edgier stuff. I mean, I think it's inevitable that people seeking to understand a movement select the similarities rather than the differences between exponents. That drives you towards the mean — the mainstream. New writers imitate that,

and before you know it, the energy's gone, because it lay in the creative tensions between the different exponents.

His response shows a distinct suspicion of the rise of both the conventional and commercial frameworks which have tended to define new 'waves' of writing historically and which would go on to attempt to define the so-called 'New Weird'. He felt that if he didn't speak up then he would have left it to others to describe what exactly it was that he was writing. And he believed that in and of itself would enervate the work.

But in describing the discussions that took place on that message board, Jonathan McCalmont said something that struck me as a sort of remedy to this:

> Every cultural entity (be it a genre, a sub-genre, a scene, a movement, or a school) is born of a particular place and time ... a sudden awareness that the wider culture has changed and that the old tools are no longer up to the job.

McCalmont suggested that the New Weird encapsulated one of those moments.

But where are we now?

Much has happened in the years since those debates and there are signs that weird fiction has been codified in exactly the way Harrison feared it would be. This anthology by definition is one of those forces for codification, attempting to sum up what weird fiction is in order to assess what is 'the best'. The best of what? The best of that which is mixed and hybrid, the best of that which defies easy categorization, the best of what ought to remain unnamed. So — no new labels. No New New Weird or Post New Weird. Just weird.

A year ago I would have said there was a danger that weird fiction will — or has already begun to — lose its edge, moving from innocence to plausibility to decadence, according to the formulation of Joanna Russ, in which originally distinct ideas and voices have become assimilated to the point of stale repetition.

And yet I believe we are in one of those moments of rapid re-imagining when the old tools of writing no longer seem up to the job.

The language of weird fiction speaks to the irrationality of our present, foundering systems. Whereas these stories have typically looked outward to generate their horror, from the undeniable xenophobia of some of Lovecraft's writing to the misogyny embraced by the slasher flicks of the 70s; but it could just as easily look inward. To be horrified by oneself, to feel a disconnection from what is labeled 'traditional' or 'natural' or 'essential' is a vital step toward embracing a radical empathy with what might have heretofore been labeled as Other. This is work that weird fiction can do.

The stories within this volume were published in 2016. Many of them were almost certainly written before the upheavals which I have been talking about, yet each in my mind embodies the spirit of upheaval and revelation, madness, despair, horror and also, sometimes, forgiveness, accommodation and change that seem to mark our apocalyptic moment. Among these writers are many names you may not recognise, and this is, to my mind, a good thing. They are writers from different countries, different languages, and different traditions. Many of these writers may not consider themselves to be weird writers in the strictest of terms and that as well is a good thing. As the editor of a volume that sets out to define the genre I confess I have the same reservations that M. John Harrison had in 2003: that weird fiction has on the one hand become too stable, too easily recognizable, and on the other so diffuse that the term no longer has any meaning at all. There is a danger with labels, but also an opportunity.

We are living in *weird* times. As I write, a snap election in the UK has just shocked the nation with another upending of the pollsters' predictions and the future seems very uncertain. In moments such as this, time itself seems out of joint. We need new tools to interrogate our present moment. We need a new language to understand it, to articulate our concerns, our hopes, our dreams — our possibilities. The writers within this volume have been, first and foremost, witnesses to their world. Their stories suggest a new language, not only for weird fiction, but for a contemporary fiction that looks for new answers in unexpected places.

It is up to us to embrace this new language, knowing that to make an end is also to make a beginning.

BIBLIOGRAPHY

SEX, DEATH AND THE MAN-OMELET IN 'THE SPECIALIST'S HAT'

James, M. R. 'Oh, Whistle and I'll Come to You, My Lad.' In *Great Horror Stories: Tales by Stoker, Poe, Lovecraft and Others*. Ed. John Grafton. Mineola, NY: Dover Publications, 2006.

Kay, Sarah. *Slavoj Žižek: A Critical Introduction*. Cambridge: Polity, 2003. Print.

Kelly, James Patrick and John Kessel, eds. *Feeling Very Strange: The Slipstream Anthology*. Francisco: Tachyon Publications, 2006. Print.

Lacan, Jacques. *The Seminar, Book XI, The Four Fundamental Concepts of Psychoanalysis*. Eds. Richard Feldstein, Bruce Fink and Maire Jaanus. Albany, NY: State University of New York Press, 1995. Print.

Link, Kelly. 'The Specialist's Hat.' *Event Horizon* November 1998. Reprinted in *Stranger Things Happen*. Brooklyn, NY: Small Beer Press, 2001. Print.

Lovecraft, H. P. *The Call of Cthulhu and Other Weird Stories*. Ed. S. T. Joshi. London: Penguin, 1999. Print.

Noys, Benjamin. 'The Horror of the Real: Žižek's Modern Gothic.' *International Journal of Zizek Studies* 4 (2010). <http://zizekstudies.org/index.php/ijzs/article/viewFile/274/372>

Žižek, Slavoj. 'Troubles with the Real: Lacan as a Viewer of Alien.' Lacan.com. 2009. http://www.lacan.com/essays/?p=180

THE ONLY LIGHTS ARE HEADLIGHTS

King, Stephen. *Danse Macabre*. New York: Hodder & Stoughton, 2006. Electronic.

King, Stephen. *The Dead Zone*. New York: New York: Doubleday & Company, 1979. Print.

King, Stephen. *It*. New York: Viking Press, 1986. Print.

King, Stephen. 'The Man in the Black Suit.' In *The Weird: A Compendium of Strange and Dark Stories*. Ed. Ann VanderMeer and Jeff VanderMeer. New York: Corvus, 2011. Electronic.

King, Stephen. *Revival*. New York: Hodder & Stoughton, 2014. Print.

King, Stephen. *Salem's Lot*. New York: Doubleday & Company, 1975. Print.

MacDonald, Helen. *H is for Hawk*. London: Vintage, 2015. Electronic.

Sometimes They Come Back. Dir. Tom McLoughlin. 1991. Based on a short story by Stephen King: 'Sometimes They Come Back.' *Cavalier*. March, 1974. Reprinted in *Night Shift*. New York: Doubleday & Company, 1978.

SURVIVAL STRATEGIES FOR WEIRD TIMES

Collings, Michael R. and Stephen E. Fabian. *The Stephen King Phenomenon*. Starmont House, 1987.

Gordon, Joan. 'Reveling in Genre: An Interview with China Miéville.' *Science Fiction Studies* 30 (2003): 91.

Harrison, M. John (u/Biomancer). 'A Short Essay by the Great Sci-Fi Author M. John Harrison About Why Storytelling Must Take Precedence Over Worldbuilding.' *Reddit*, December 14, 2014. https://www.reddit.com/r/writing/comments/2p80gc/a_short_essay_by_the_great_scifi_author_m_john/

Karyn Kusama, dir. *The Invitation*. 2015; New York City, New York: Gamechanger Films. Blu-ray Disc, 1080p.

Kelly, James P. and John Kessel, eds. *Feeling Very Strange: The Slipstream Anthology*. San Francisco: Tachyon Publications, 2006.

King, Stephen. *On Writing: A Memoir of the Craft*. New York: Scribner, 2000.

Lovecraft, H.P. *The Annotated Supernatural Horror in Literature*. Edited by S.T. Joshi. New York: Hippocampus Press, 2000.

Lovecraft, H.P. 'The Call of Cthulhu.' In *The Call of Cthulhu and Other Weird Stories*. Edited by S.T. Joshi. New York: Penguin Classics, 2002.

Luckhurst, Roger. 'The Weird: A Dis/orientation.' *Textual Practice* 31, no. 6, (2017): 1041–61.

Marshall, Helen. 'Introduction.' In *The Year's Best Weird Fiction*, Vol. 4. Edited by Helen Marshall and Michael Kelly. Toronto: Undertow Publications, 2017.

Marshall, Helen. 'The Only Lights are Headlights.' *Weird Fiction Review*, August 10, 2016. http://weirdfictionreview.com/2016/08/101-weird-writers-43-stephen-king/

Morton, Timothy. *Hyperobjects: Philosophy and Ecology after the End of the World*. Minneapolis: University of Minnesota Press, 2013.

Sterling. Bruce. 'Catscan.' *SF Eye #5*. July 1989. http://indbooks.in/mirror1/?p=311829.

Stross, Charlie. 'Why I Barely Read SF These Days.' *Charlie's Diary*, February 6, 2018. http://www.antipope.org/charlie/blog-static/2018/02/why-i-barely-read-sf-these-day.html

Takashi Shimizu, dir. *Ju-on: The Grudge*. 2003; Akasaka, Minato, Tokyo, Japan: Pioneer LDC. Blu-ray Disc, 1080p HD.

Todorov, Tzvetan. *The Fantastic: A Structural Approach to a Literary Genre*. Translated by Richard Howard. Ithaca, New York: Cornell University Press, 1973.

VanderMeer, Ann and Jeff VanderMeer, eds. *The Weird: A Compendium of Strange and Dark Stories*. New York: Tor Books, 2012

Von Weber, Carl Maria. 'On the Opera Undine.' In *Allgemeine Musikalische Zeitung* 19 (1817): 201–208. Reprinted in *Source Readings in Music History: The Romantic Era*. Translated by Oliver Strunk. London: Norton, 1965.

Weinstock, Jeffrey Andrew. 'The New Weird.' In *New Directions in Popular Fiction: Genre, Reproduction, Distribution*. Edited by Ken Gelder, 177–200. Basingstoke: Palgrave Macmillan, 2016.

'A FLARE OF LIGHT OR THE GREAT CLOMPING FOOT OF NERDISM?'

Anders, CJ 2013 '7 Deadly Sins of Worldbuilding', *Gizmodo* (August 2): http://io9. gizmodo.com/7-deadly-sins-of-worldbuilding-998817537 (accessed 23 October, 2019)

Bakker, RS 2008 'New R. Scott Bakker Q&Q', *Pat's Fantasy Hotlist* (January 21): http://fantasyhotlist.blogspot.com/2008/01/new-r-scott-bakker-q.html (accessed on 23 October, 2019)

Ballard, JG 2017 [1962] 'Which Way to Inner Space?', in R Latham (ed) *Science Fiction Criticism: An Anthology of Essential Writings*, Bloomsbury, London

Baudrillard J 1994 *Simulacra and Simulation*, SF Glaser (trans), The University of Michigan Press, Ann Arbor

Bould, M, et al (eds) 2005 *Parietal Games: Critical Writings by and on M. John Harrison*, Science Fiction Foundation, London

Butler, A 2003 'Thirteen Ways of Looking at the British Boom', *Science Fiction Studies* 30: https://www.depauw.edu/sfs/pioneers/butler91.htm (accessed 23 October, 2019)

Darlington, A 1983 'The New and Newer Worlds of M. John Harrison', *Arts Yorkshire* (September): http://sanfransys.com/homepages/harrison/harrison4.htm (accessed 23 October, 2019)

Datlow, E (ed) 2015 *Lovecraft Unbound*, Dark Horse Books, New York

Datlow, E (ed) 2016 *Children of Lovecraft*, Dark Horse Books, New York

Fraser, G 2019 'Viriconium Ghostwalk', in R Williams et al *M. John Harrison: Critical Essays*, Glyphi Limited, London

Gaiman, N 2005 'Introduction', in MJ Harrison *Viriconium*, New York, Bantam

Guran, P (ed) 2016 *The Mammoth Book of Original Cthulhu: New Lovecraftian Fiction*, Mammoth Books, New York

Macfarlane, R 2013 'Robert Macfarlane: rereading Climbers by M John Harrison', *The Guardian* (May 10): https://www.theguardian.com/books/2013/may/10/robert-macfarlane-rereading-climbers (accessed 23 October, 2019)

Mathijs, E 2006 *The Lord of the Rings: Popular Culture in Global Context*, Wallflower Press, London

Moorcock, M 2008 [1978] 'Epic Pooh', in H Bloom (ed) *The Lord of the Rings*, New Edition, Bloom's Literary Criticism, New York

Harrison, MJ 1975 'Sweet Analytics', in H Bailey (ed) *New World 9*, Corgi, London

Harrison, MJ 1989 *Climbers: A Novel*, Gollancz, London

Harrison, MJ 1992 [1989] 'The Profession of Fiction', in M Jakubowski and E James (eds) *The Profession of Science Fiction: Writers on Their Craft and Ideas*, The Macmillan Press, Ltd. London

Harrison, MJ 2001 'What It Might be Like to Live in Viriconium', (October 15): http://www.fantasticmetropolis.com/i/viriconium/ (accessed 23 October, 2019)

Harrison, MJ 2005 *Viriconium*, New York, Bantam

Harrison, MJ 2005 1971 [1971] *The Pastel City*, in MJ Harrison *Viriconium*, New York, Bantam

Harrison, MJ 2005 [1980] *A Storm of Wings*, in MJ Harrison *Viriconium*, New York, Bantam

Harrison, MJ 2007a 'Licensed Settings' (January 18): https://web.archive.org/web/20080301191612/http://uzwi.wordpress.com/2007/01/18/licensed-settings/ (accessed 23 October, 2019)

Harrison, MJ 2007b 'Very Afraid' (January 27): https://web.archive.org/web/20080205000327/http://uzwi.wordpress.com/2007/01/27/very-afraid/ (accessed 23 October, 2019)

Harrison, MJ 2007c 'Worldbuilding: Further Notes' (December 21): https://web.archive.org/web/20080203094611/http://uzwi.wordpress.com/worldbuilding-further-notes/ (accessed 23 October, 2019)

Harrison, MJ 2012 'I'm Not Against Worldbuilding...' (April 19): https://ambientehotel.wordpress.com/2012/04/19/im-not-against-worldbuilding/ (accessed 24 October, 2019)

Harrison MJ et al 2016 'New Worlds: An Interview with M. John Harrison', *Former People* (April 16): https://formerpeople.wordpress.com/2016/04/16/new-worlds-an-interview-with-m-john-harrison/ (accessed on 23 October, 2019)

Holling, CS 2001 'Understanding the Complexity of Economic, Ecological, and Social systems', *Ecosystems* 4, 390-405

Jenkins, H 2006 *Convergence Culture: Where Old and New Media Collide*, NYU Press, New York

Latham, R 2019 [2005] 'A Young Man's Journey to Ladbroke Grove: M. John Harrison and the Evolution of the New Wave in Britain', in R Williams et al *M. John Harrison: Critical Essays*, Glyphi Limited, London

Lombardo, T 2018 *Science Fiction: The Evolutionary Mythology of the Future Vol. 1* Changemakers Books, Alesford, UK

Macdonald, G 2004 [1890] 'The Fantastic Imagination', in D Sander (ed) *Fantastic Literature: A Critical Reader*, Praeger, Westport CT

Marshall, H 2017 'Introduction', in H Marshall and M Kelly (eds) *The Year's Best Weird Fiction, Vol. 4*, Undertow Publications, Toronto

McCalmont, J 2016 'Nothing Beside Remains: A History of the New Weird', Big Echo: Critical SF: http://www.bigecho.org/nothing-beside-remains (accessed 23 October, 2019)

Miéville, C 2000 *Perdido Street Station*, MacMillan, London

Miéville, C 2002a 'Middle Earth Meets Middle England' *Socialist Review*: http://

socialistreview.org.uk/259/tolkien-middle-earth-meets-middle-england (accessed 23 October, 2019)

Miéville, C 2002b 'Debate' *China Miéville* (February 25): https://web.archive.org/web/20050219024912/https://www.panmacmillan.com/Features/China/debate.htm, (accessed via the Way Back Machine on February 19, 2005)

Miéville, C 2002c *The Scar*, MacMillan, London

Miéville, C 2004 [2002] 'Introduction to *Marxism and Fantasy*', in D Sander (ed) *Fantastic Literature: A Critical Reader*, Praeger, Westport CT

Miéville, C 2004 *Iron Council*, MacMillan, London

Miéville, C 2005 'With One Bound We are Free: Pulp, Fantasy and Revolution', *Out of the Crooked Timber of Humanity, No Straight Thing Was Ever Made* (January 11): http://crookedtimber.org/2005/01/11/with-one-bound-we-are-free-pulp-fantasy-and-revolution/?fbclid=IwAR1v_OMzQG53mr-W6fd42f72kW2RLQ3D5FkPNK88GGw8bdEAD8hSAHfyXyUQ (accessed 23 October, 2019)

Miéville, C 2011 'M.R. James and the Quantum Vampire Weird; Hauntological: Versus and/or and and/or or?' *Weird Fiction Review* (November 29): http://weirdfictionreview.com/2011/11/m-r-james-and-the-quantum-vampire-by-china-mieville/ (accessed 23 October, 2019)

Moher, A 2010 'Review: *The Pastel City* by M. John Harrison', (October 18): https://www.tor.com/2010/10/18/review-the-pastel-city-by-m-john-harrison/ (accessed 23 October, 2019)

Morton, T 2013 *Hyperobjects: Philosophy and Ecology after the End of the World*, University of Minnesota Press, Minneapolis, MN

Nicolay, S 2011 'Dogme 2011 for Weird Fiction', *Weird Fiction Review* (November 21): http://weirdfictionreview.com/2011/11/dogme-2011-for-weird-fiction-by-scott-nicolay/ (accessed 23 October, 2019)

Pak, C 2019 'Something That Looked Like a Woman Partly like a Cat': Deliquescence, Hybridity and the Animal in the Empty Space Trilogy' in R Williams et al 2019 *M. John Harrison: Critical Essays*, Glyphi Limited, London

Robson, Justin 2003 'June 13 – 05:44 pm' in 'New Weird 4.5: the net on both sides', *Kathryn Cramer*: https://www.kathryncramer.com/kathryn_cramer/the-new-weird-p-5.html (accessed 23 October, 2019)

Sheppard, R 2003 *The Necessity of Poetics*, Edge Hill Edition, Edge Hill

St-Denis, P 2007 'Be Afraid...Be Very Afraid...', *Pat's Fantasy Hotlist* (February 5): http://fantasyhotlist.blogspot.com/2007/02/be-afraid-be-very-afraid.html (accessed 23 October, 2019)

Stross, C 2008 'Why I barely read SF these days', *Charlie's Diary* (February 6): http://www.antipope.org/charlie/blog-static/2018/02/why-i-barely-read-sf-these-day.html, (accessed 23 October, 2019)

Šust, M et al 2008 'European Editor Perspectives on the New Weird', in J VanderMeer and A VanderMeer (eds) *The New Weird*, Tachyon Publications, San Francisco

Taylor, AU 2017 *Patricia A. McKillip and the Art of Fantasy World-Building*, Critical Explorations in Science Fiction and Fantasy 60, McFarland & Company, Inc., New York

Tolkien, JRR 2008 [1945] *On Fairy-Stories*, V Flieger and DA Anderson (eds), HarperCollins, New York

VanderMeer, J and A VanderMeer (eds) 2008 *The New Weird*, Tachyon Publications, San Francisco

VanderMeer, J and A VanderMeer (eds) 2011 *The Weird Compendium*, Tor, New York

VanderMeer, J 2013 *Wonderbook: The Illustrated Guide to Creating Imaginative Fiction*, Abrams Image, New York

Wolfe, G and A Beamer 2011 'Peter Straub and the New Horror', in G Wolfe *Evaporating Genres: Essays on Fantastic Literature*, Wesleyan University Press, New York, 151-163

Wolf, MJP 2012 *Building Imaginary Worlds: The Theory and History of Subcreation*, Routledge, New York and London

Wolf, MJP (ed) 2017 *The Routledge Companion to Imaginary Worlds*, Routledge, New York and London

Zaidi, L 2009 'Worldbuilding in Science Fiction, Foresight and Design', *Journal of Futures Studies*, 23: 15–26

ABOUT THE AUTHOR

Helen Marshall's creative writing aims to bring the past into conversation with the present. After receiving a PhD from the Centre for Medieval Studies at the University of Toronto, she completed a postdoctoral fellowship at the University of Oxford investigating literature written during the time of the Black Death. Her first collection of fiction, *Hair Side, Flesh Side*, which won the Sydney J Bounds Award in 2013, emerged from this work as a book historian. Rather than taking the long view of history, her second collection, *Gifts for the One Who Comes After*, negotiated very personal issues of legacy and tradition, creating myth-infused worlds where "love is as liable to cut as to cradle, childhood is a supernatural minefield, and death is 'the slow undoing of beautiful things'" (*Quill&Quire*, starred review). It won the World Fantasy Award and the Shirley Jackson Award in 2015. Her debut novel *The Migration* was one of The Guardian's top science fiction books of the year. It was shortlisted for two British Fantasy Awards as well as the Sunburst Award for Canadian Literature of the Fantastic.

She is a Senior Lecturer of Creative Writing at The University of Queensland.

twitter.com/manuscriptgal

THANK YOU FOR BUYING THIS BRAIN JAR PRESS CHAPBOOK

To receive special offers, bonus content, and info on new releases and other great reads, visit us online at www.BrainJarPress.com

www.ingramcontent.com/pod-product-compliance
Lightning Source LLC
Chambersburg PA
CBHW030307100526
44590CB00012B/553